American Holy Days

American Holy Days

The Heart and Soul of Our National Holidays

BOARDMAN W. KATHAN

RESOURCE *Publications* · Eugene, Oregon

AMERICAN HOLY DAYS
The Heart and Soul of Our National Holidays

Resource Publications
An Imprint of Wipf and Stock Publishers
199 W. 8th Ave., Suite 3
Eugene, OR 97401

www.wipfandstock.com

PAPERBACK ISBN: 978-1-5326-1455-2
HARDCOVER ISBN: 978-1-5326-1457-6
EBOOK ISBN: 978-1-5326-1456-9

Manufactured in the U.S.A.   AUGUST 1, 2017

Grateful acknowledgement is expressed for permission to use the following material from published sources:

To Carl Wendell Hines, Jr., for permission to use part of his poem "Now That He Is Safely Dead," from the book *Hold Fast to Dreams,* edited by Arna Bontemps (1969).

To the Reconstructionist Press for permission to use an excerpt from the chapter on Columbus Day in the book *The Faith of America: Prayers, Readings and Songs for the Celebration of American Holidays,* edited by Rabbi Mordecai Kaplan and others (1951).

To Joseph L. Gomez for permission to use part of the letter "Dear Josie" from his book *Not In Vain: A Story of A Soldier* (2007).

Every effort was made during six months (without success) to attain permission to use brief excerpts from a guest editorial in a 1961 *LIFE* magazine, an essay in a 1989 *TIME* magazine, and an article in a 1957 *Ladies Home Journal.*

Contents

CONTENTS

Introduction

WITH THE TITLE, "EAT Turkey, Become American," there appeared in *The New York Times* on November 24, 2014, an article by Marie Myung-Ok Lee about a Korean family in northern Minnesota letting go of their own national cuisine and adopting the American tradition of Thanksgiving. She described it as her "parents' yearly recommitment ceremony to America." This story can be repeated many times as even the most recent immigrants to these shores are immersed in the country's holidays as a way to become accepted as citizens. "Eat Turkey, Become American."[1]

Our national holidays have become an occasion for trips to the mall to seek out bargains and sales. The most common and pervasive message of the holidays is found in the advertising on television and elsewhere, that it is time to buy the latest electronic gadgets, furniture, and other merchandise. The message seems to be: "Buy a car, Be patriotic."

The extended three-day weekend with a day-off on Monday has provided additional time for recreational pursuits and leisure. Memorial Day begins the summer unofficially and Labor Day closes it, with ample time to fire up the grill, take a trip to the beach, the lake, or the mountains. For those who are able, the goal is "Get away. Do your duty as a citizen."

Everyone has a favorite holiday, whether it is Thanksgiving with turkey and all the trimmings, the Fourth of July with fireworks, or Memorial Day with parades or solemn processions. The Harris Poll revealed in 2011 that Christmas was the number one favorite holiday, followed by Thanksgiving. The only other patriotic holidays to make the top ten list were the Fourth of July, Memorial Day, and Labor Day. The Harris Poll reported that "Americans often gather with friends or family for holidays, taking part in rituals and traditions as diverse as eating special dishes, watching a football game, gift giving or reciting meaningful prayers and songs." These are the sacred or almost-sacred rituals of family and community life.

1. Lee, *New York Times* (Nov. 27, 2014) A35

Everyone has memories and stories to tell: of a special trip, a family reunion, a concert, bringing flowers to a cemetery, honoring veterans, recitation of the "Gettysburg Address," a naturalization ceremony. The mayor of
my home town, Bob Chatfield, can remember for over thirty-eight years of-
ficiating at the Memorial Day exercises on the town Green, which included
honoring Gold Star mothers, laying wreaths at a Civil War monument, and
the reciting of "In Flanders Field." Carroll Brown of the West Haven Black
Coalition in Connecticut can remember organizing the large, multi-racial
celebration of the life of Martin Luther King, Jr., every year since 1986,
when King's birthday was added to the national calendar.

America's national, patriotic holidays honor events and persons which
have shaped American history and identity. This book does not include religious holidays like Christmas, but it does add Flag Day and Constitution
Day, which are not legal days off from work or school, but which nonetheless
recognize important events such as the creation of the first American flag
in 1777 and the adoption of the U.S. Constitution in 1787. It also includes
George Washington's Birthday, which had been moved to the third Monday
of February by act of the U.S. Congress in 1971, and is known popularly as
Presidents' Day. Abraham Lincoln's Birthday is included as an Appendix
since it is celebrated in many places. These patriotic days become national,
not just federal, only when they are adopted by the individual states.

The title "American Holy Days" reflects three levels of meaning and
understanding. The first and most obvious is that the word "holiday" is
derived from Old English for "holy days." The second is the fact that people
follow rituals or traditions on holidays that border on faithful devotion, like
the Korean family in northern Minnesota; they carry out some activities
"religiously."

The third level of understanding is not as familiar: namely, that these
patriotic holidays have been called the holy days of American civil religion.
The sociologist Robert Bellah wrote an essay in the Winter 1967 issue of
Daedalus, journal of the American Academy of Arts and Sciences, in which
he claimed that "there actually exists alongside of and rather clearly differ-
entiated from the churches an elaborate and well-institutionalized civil religion in America," and that it has "beliefs, rituals and symbols." According
to Bellah, this American civil religion is "not the worship of the American
nation, but an understanding of the American experience in the light of
ultimate and universal reality."[2] Benjamin Franklin used the term, "public

2. Bellah, *Daedalus*, 96 (1) 18

religion," in contrast with the private religions of Judaism, Christianity, Islam, and others.

The concept of American civil religion is becoming more familiar; Wikipedia has started to use the term in its entries on national holidays. In 2017 the Yale sociologist Philip Gorski has written a book, *American Covenant: A History of Civil Religion from the Puritans to the Present*. He acknowledged that rituals are "important to civil religion, such as ceremonies, commemorations, parades, and so on." He was very blunt: "America's civic holidays, like so much of its public life, have been gradually colonized by consumer capitalism."[3]

I was asked to write an article on the subject for the *Religion Teacher's Journal* in 1975, in which I defined American civil religion as "the peculiar blending of patriotism and piety that has characterized our public life as a nation and our self-understanding as a people with a special purpose and destiny in the world."[4] This civil or public religion has acquired a set of beliefs, rituals, symbols, saints, scriptures, and holy days. Many books have been written about the pantheon of heroes, the flag and other symbols, the shrines and memorials in this country's history.

Random House has published two books on the subject. Pauline Maier, professor at MIT, wrote the book *American Scripture: Making the Declaration of Independence* in 1997. Her purpose was to explore how the document was created and how it became a sacred text for the American people. In 2006 Jon Meacham, editor of *Newsweek*, wrote *American Gospel: God, the Founding Fathers, and the Making of a Nation*. Meacham stated that the purpose of his book was "to explore the role faith has played in the Republic and to illustrate how the Founding Fathers left us with a tradition in which we could talk and think about God and politics without descending into discord and division."[5] President Obama said the nation has a "common creed."

There have been several books about our national, patriotic holy days. One is *Celebrations: The Complete Book of American Holidays* by Robert J. Myers, published in cooperation with the editors of Hallmark Cards by Doubleday and Company in 1972. The book briefly covered forty-five "Widely Observed Holidays" and fifteen "Holidays Briefly Noted." Included,

---

3. Gorski, *American Covenant,* 14, 228

4. Kathan, *Religion Teacher's Journal,* 9 (7) 16

5. Meacham, *American Gospel,* 16

of course, were many religious days and popular ones for selling greeting cards, such as Valentine's Day, Mother's Day, Father's Day, and Hallowe'en.

A second book is *America's Public Holidays, 1865–1920* by Ellen M. Litwicki, published by the Smithsonian Institution Press in 2000. This volume was based on her doctoral dissertation and covered more than twenty-five holidays which emerged between the Civil War and 1920. She has chronicled the efforts of many groups to try to get holidays recognized.

A third book is *Red, White, and Blue Letter Days: An American Calendar* by Matthew Dennis, which was published in 2002 by Cornell University Press. Dennis explored over twenty-five holidays and has concentrated on the politics of holiday-making and observing, using them to push special agendas. He went into great detail to explain the exclusion of African-Americans, women, Native Americans, Jews and Mormons from full participation and their reaction to the development of specific holidays. In his book Dennis stated that our three-day holiday weekends are devoted to leisure, consumption or consumerism, and historical amnesia.

The purpose of my own book is to deal with that historical amnesia, restore the meaning of eleven patriotic holidays (including Lincoln's Birthday) and inspire renewed ways of celebration, commemoration, and observance. This will help us recall our history, reclaim our values and traditions, and restore a sense of community. Each chapter will look at the origins and purpose of the holiday, its evolution or development in American history, some books and research about it, its relevance for today, and any spiritual dimensions.

It is repeated often at the annual Academy Awards show that movies can tell stories that inspire us, and so it is with the stories of our country. Like the movies that are nominated for awards, the narratives in our country's history say much about the human condition and the resilience of the human spirit. In spite of the tragic stories of the slavery of African-Americans, the annihilation of Native Americans, the exclusion of women, ethnic and national groups, or of people with challenging conditions or different sexual orientation, there has been progress toward full citizenship and participatory democracy. These stories can bring us together as we celebrate these patriotic holy days. There is much that divides us in terms of party affiliation, ideology, beliefs, and values, but there is also much that unites us in the stories of how our country was founded and shaped. It has been said that in time of stress and conflict the celebration of our national holidays can help to bring us together.

This book has a bias, namely that people throughout American history have believed that God worked in their lives and in the life of the nation. The Pilgrim fathers and mothers felt that God had led them across a sea from a place of oppression to a "promised land, flowing with milk and honey." George Washington, in his 1789 Thanksgiving proclamation, acknowledged the providence of Almighty God. In the fourth stanza of our national anthem, the "Star Spangled Banner," Francis Scott Key wrote: "In God is our Trust." Abraham Lincoln spoke at Gettysburg of a nation "under God." John F. Kennedy concluded his inaugural address with the words, "here on earth God's work must truly be our own."

This book seeks to correct or clarify long-standing myths and traditions that surround the holidays. For example, the First Thanksgiving in the new world was not celebrated in 1621 by the Pilgrims and their Wampanoag visitors. Betsy Ross did not design the first American flag in 1776. Of course, Columbus did not discover America, but did bring civilizations together that had been separated for millennia and started what has been called the "Columbian exchange." Labor Day was established in 1894 to appease the labor movement after President Grover Cleveland had sent in the army and marshals to quell the Pullman Company strike.

The book deals with controversial issues. For decades people have debated the religions of Washington and Lincoln, whether Washington was a Deist like Thomas Jefferson. The "separation of church and state" was incorporated in the U.S. Constitution even before the First Amendment of the Bill of Rights was ratified. Washington supported this separation with one possible exception, but he set precedents for the invocation of God in public life. The Constitution did not establish a "Christian nation."

David McCullough, author of best-selling biographies, has said that our students are "historically illiterate," that they forget what made our nation great, what it has accomplished, why so many seek and sacrifice to come to these shores. He added that adults share in the responsibility, because they have failed to pass on to the next generation the values and traditions of our country. Younger citizens often take for granted the "blessings of liberty," which they enjoy. Knowledge of the Declaration of Independence and the U.S. Constitution is lacking. Little is known of the lives of Martin Luther King, Jr., Abraham Lincoln, George Washington, and Christopher Columbus. There is great misunderstanding of the original meaning and purpose of Memorial Day, Labor Day, and Veterans Day. The significance of Thanksgiving has become almost lost in the rush toward Christmas and is now threatened by the invasion of the "Black Friday" shopping madness.

This book is not a textbook for schools, but a supplementary resource for dealing with the well-known holidays that recall and bring to life important parts of American history. The study of the nation's holidays may be a more interesting approach to the study of history. For those who wonder how a book on "holy days" and religious references could be used in public schools, the U.S. Supreme Court made very clear in its 1962 *Engel v. Vitale* decision:

> "that school children should not be discouraged from expressing love for our country by reciting historical documents such as the Declaration of Independence, which contain references to the deity, or by singing officially espoused anthems which include the composer's professions of faith in a Supreme Being, or . . . many manifestations in our public life of belief in God."[6]

This is not a book of sermons similar to the 1976 volume edited by Alton M. Motter, *Preaching on National Holidays*, nor is it a resource for worship services like *The Faith of America: Readings, Songs, and Prayers for the Celebration of American Holidays*, edited by Rabbi Mordecai Kaplan and others and published in 1951. Leaders and members of faith communities have their own religious holy days, but the civil calendar provides a rich opportunity for worship services and educational programs. Congregations need to be assured that American civil or public religion is not idolatry, nationalism, or worship of the state, but rather an understanding of the rightful place of a transcendent God in our nation's life and work. Speaking for Christian churches, William Zito said it well in his 1987 doctoral thesis at Hartford Seminary: "it is time for us, the religious community, to reclaim our American holidays and either restore them to their original intent or fill them with a religious dimension, which lifts them out of the superficial, making them significant and relevant to our lives."[7]

Besides schools and religious institutions, there is a great need for a book on our national, patriotic holidays for all American citizens, and for those who would like to become citizens. Newcomers to our shores are quickly caught up in the cycle of holidays and want to learn more about their beginnings and significance.

6. Engel v. Vitale, 370 US 421 (1962) 435
7. Zito, "Thanksgiving Day," (1987) 33

There are those who would say that there are no national holidays, only federal ones. This may be technically true, since only the U.S. Congress can declare holidays for all federal agencies, the District of Columbia, and American territories. However, these holidays have become national through proclamations in all the states, and are recognized by most people as national.

This book is not an academic tome, but one for the general public. Many books and much research about the holidays are summarized, and there is a Selective Bibliography for each chapter.

This book would not be possible without the help of many people: the librarians of the Prospect and Cheshire, Connecticut, Public Libraries, the Interlibrary Loan, the Connecticut State Library in Hartford, and the libraries of Yale University in New Haven. I am especially indebted to Joan Duffy and Kevin Crawford, archivists at Yale Divinity School library.

Along the way I met and was inspired by authors like: Andrew Young, aide to Dr. King, Congressman, U.N. Ambassador and Mayor of Atlanta; Mary Thompson of the Mt. Vernon Ladies Association; Marla Miller of the University of Massachusetts, Amherst; James McPherson, emeritus professor at Princeton University; Harry Stout of Yale University; and Michael Burlingame, emeritus professor of Connecticut College, now at the University of Illinois.

I am very grateful to those who read the manuscript and made suggestions and corrections: the Rev. Dr. James Scott, a classmate of mine at Yale and retired minister; Donald Schellhardt, a retired attorney; Louise MacCormack, a retired English teacher; and John White, who served as my literary agent. Also, thanks to Marilyn Wanek for her assistance. Finally, I am especially grateful to my daughter, Nancy Lee Kathan, for her computer expertise and tech support.

Rev. Boardman W. Kathan
Prospect, Connecticut
July 4, 2017

CHAPTER 1

A Drum Major For Justice

MARTIN LUTHER KING, JR. DAY

"Now that he is safely dead
let us praise him
build monuments to his glory
sing hosannas to his name.
Dead men make
such convenient heroes. They
cannot rise
to challenge the images
we would fashion from their lives.
And besides,
it is easier to build monuments
than to make a better world." [1]

THIS IS THE BEGINNING of a poem by Carl Wendell Hines, Jr., that first appeared in the book, *Hold Fast to Dreams,* edited by Arna Bontemps and published in 1969, a year after the assassination of Martin Luther King, Jr. The poem was reprinted in 1976 and published in India by the Writers Workshop in a slim volume of poetic tributes to King entitled *Drum Major for a Dream.* In addition, it was quoted by Vincent Harding and became the inspiration for the title of his book, *Martin Luther King: The Inconvenient Hero.* Harding maintained that we suffer from "national amnesia" and have

1. Bontemps, ed., *Hold Fast to Dreams,* 147.

fashioned observances of the day in King's honor that reflect the sunshine of his famous "I Have A Dream" speech at the 1963 March on Washington and ignore the shadows of the last years of his life. The metaphor called attention to efforts "to manage, market and domesticate him," while avoiding his search for economic and social justice, his identification with the poor people, his opposition to the Vietnam War, and his struggle against racism, militarism, and materialism. According to Harding, we have made King a "smoothed-off, respectable national hero," with whom we can be comfortable. [2]

Carl Wendell Hines, Jr., wrote, "It is easier to build monuments than to make a better world." In 2011 the Martin Luther King Jr. National Memorial was dedicated in Washington, DC, on the tidal basin not far from the memorials for Thomas Jefferson, Abraham Lincoln, and Franklin Roosevelt. Many years in planning and fund-raising, the multi-million dollar King Memorial was organized by the National Memorial Project Foundation, authorized by the U.S. Congress. The memorial signaled the addition of Dr. King to the national pantheon, if he were not already there through a national holiday. What made the King memorial unique was not only that it honored a Baptist preacher who had never held public office, but the leading voice of the Civil Rights Movement in the twentieth century, a winner of the Nobel Peace Prize, an outstanding orator, and the only African-American.

What Lincoln had done in the nineteenth century, reminding Americans of their founding documents and chartered freedoms, King had done in the twentieth century, confronting Jim Crow laws that had reduced Americans of African descent to second-class citizenship. He was born in a country where people, because of the color of their skin, had to ride in the back of the bus, were refused service at lunch counters, could not freely vote or serve on a jury, and were humiliated every day by segregated water fountains, waiting rooms, trains and buses, hotels and restaurants, parks and playgrounds, libraries, and theatres. King appealed to the "unalienable rights" of the Declaration of Independence and to the amendments to the Constitution which called for "equal justice under law."

In his most famous "I have a dream" speech in front of the Lincoln Memorial on August 28, 1963, he challenged America to "live out the true meaning of its creed—we hold these truths to be self-evident, that all men

2. Harding, *Martin Luther King*, 23

are created equal."[3] The tragedy was that he was cut down in his prime, before he was forty years old, by an assassin's bullet. Like that "Great Soul" of India, Mohandas Gandhi, this American prophet of non-violence and civil disobedience to unjust laws died a violent death as a martyr for the cause. The story of how his birthday became a legal holiday is about as complex as the story of the man himself and it took fifteen years to achieve.

Establishing Martin Luther King Day

When he was President, Jimmy Carter recommended a holiday to honor Martin Luther King, Jr. Soon after King's assassination in 1968 a bill was submitted to Congress to create a holiday, and every year it was put on the agenda by Representatives John Conyers of Michigan and Shirley Chisholm of New York. A Senate bill was proposed by Edward Brooke of Massachusetts, which would authorize the President to offer a proclamation designating January 15 as "Martin Luther King Day," calling on people to commemorate the life and service of the Reverend Martin Luther King, Jr. The legislation went nowhere for years, and when it was finally debated in 1979 it did not receive enough votes to win passage. It is important to list some reasons it was opposed: there were those who felt that there were already too many paid federal holidays; those who felt that January 15 was too close to Christmas and New Year's Day; those who felt that the entire Civil Rights Movement should be honored, not just one man; and those who were opposed to honoring a private citizen. And there were those who were prejudiced against an African-American.

In 1983 the bill establishing Martin Luther King Jr. Day was passed, due to a number of factors. Three organizations played a role in gaining support for the legislation: the Congressional Black Caucus, formed in 1971, the Southern Christian Leadership Conference, over which King had presided; and the King Center in Atlanta. A petition was signed with six million signatures and presented to Congress; there were Civil Rights marches and demonstrations; and a prayer vigil; even Stevie Wonder was featured at a concert with a rendition of "Happy Birthday." The bill won the support of the Democratic Party leaders and of Republican leaders as well. Congressman Jack Kemp of New York voted for it, saying that he had changed his position on the vote because of the historic guarantee of human rights for all Americans.

3. Carson, *The Autobiography of Martin Luther King, Jr.,* 226

In the Senate, after a filibuster by Jesse Helms of South Carolina was ended, the body voted 78 to 22 in favor. On November 2, 1983, Ronald Reagan signed the bill into law, saying that Dr. King had awakened a sense that justice must be colorblind, and that the destiny and freedom of white and black Americans are inextricably bound together. The holiday was scheduled to fall on the third Monday of January and was observed for the first time on January 20, 1986.

That was not the end of the matter. Several states chose not to observe the day or changed its name. Arizona voted not to add the holiday to its calendar, and in protest the National Football League moved Super Bowl XXVII from Tempe, Arizona, to the Rose Bowl in Pasadena, California. New Hampshire established "Civil Rights Day" in 1991 and did not change it until eight years later. In Utah the day was called "Human Rights Day" until 2000. In Virginia it was called Lee-Jackson-King Day, combining in an incongruous way the birthday of the Civil Rights leader with two Confederate Army generals. It also became King Day in Virginia by 2000. Also, in the year 2000 South Carolina became the last state to make the day a paid holiday for State employees. In 1994 the U.S. Congress passed a bill making Martin Luther King Jr. Day a day of volunteer service in his honor. In places as far away as Israel and Japan a day to honor King has been observed.

Books on King and the Civil Rights Movement

There are hundreds of books on Martin Luther King, Jr. and the Civil Rights Movement. One author, Harvard Sitkoff, professor at the University of Massachusetts at Amherst, has appended a seventeen-page bibliographic essay to his 2008 book, *King: Pilgrimage to the Mountaintop*. Of great importance to Sitkoff was the multi-volume *Papers of Martin Luther King, Jr.,* collected and edited by Clayborne Carson, professor at Stanford University and director of the project for the King Center in Atlanta, Georgia. Coretta Scott King had enlisted Carson to edit the papers of her late husband, and the project will comprise fourteen volumes in all. This series began in 1992 with a compilation of the King's early academic work in the 1940s and early 1950s, as well as correspondence and other documents. Although King was never able to write his own autobiography, Carson has drawn upon letters, diaries, books, speeches, sermons, and recordings to put together *The Autobiography of Martin Luther King, Jr.,* published in 1998. The result is a readable, comprehensive narrative that covers King's entire life.

These works by Carson are complemented by the large volume, *A Testament of Hope: The Essential Writings and Speeches of Martin Luther King, Jr.*, edited by James Melvin Washington, professor at Union Theological Seminary in New York City, originally published in 1986. In his Introduction, Washington made clear that King belonged to a great tradition of American social reformers and dissenters, who have called attention to the country's unfulfilled promises and original ideals.

Most important, the editor has reiterated King's grounding in the strong spiritual tradition of the African-American church. King was grateful for this heritage, but was disappointed that more African-Americans had not joined the movement. He was acutely aware of how much brutality and violence had been inflicted on church congregations, how many church buildings had been burned, and how many members had suffered reprisals, beatings, and death.

Washington has repeated the five factors that King identified in bringing about a "sea change" with African-Americans: 1) migration to the urban North; 2) education of leaders at black colleges and universities, such as Fisk, Howard, Tuskegee, Virginia Union, and Morehouse; 3) improvement of the economic conditions of black Americans; 4) success of the NAACP, especially the suit brought by the Rev. Leon Oliver Brown of Topeka, Kansas, against the Board of Education, resulting in the unanimous U.S. Supreme Court decision in 1954 to desegregate public schools; and 5) the rising tide of racial consciousness and a sense of solidarity with people in Africa and Asia in their struggle for freedom and independence.

Sitkoff referred to David J. Garrow's Pulitzer Prize-winning volume, *Bearing the Cross: Martin Luther King, Jr. and the Southern Christian Leadership Conference*, as "the most masterly researched biography of King." At the time it was published in 1986, Garrow was a professor at the City University of New York and the City University Graduate Center. His interest in the subject, however, began at Wesleyan University in Middletown, Connecticut, where he did an honors thesis on King. Garrow's biography was enriched by 700 interviews with King's associates, followers, as well as opponents, access to numerous tapes and transcripts, and the recently released FBI tapes and other government documents due to the Freedom of Information Act. Included in the latter were transcripts of FBI wiretapping of King's telephone conversations. According to James Washington, "we have learned much from Garrow's gargantuan effort to preserve the humanity and historical significance of King and the SCLC."[4]

Of epic proportions are the three volumes by Taylor Branch, journalist and historian in Baltimore, Maryland. The first in the trilogy was *Parting the Waters: America in the King Years*, 1954–63, which won the Pulitzer Prize for history when it was published in 1988. This was followed by *Pillar of Fire: America in the King Years*, 1963–65, published in 1998, and *At Canaan's Edge: America in the King Years*, 1965–68, published in 2006. The trilogy began with the fascinating story of the legendary preacher, Vernon Johns, who preceded King at the Dexter Avenue Baptist Church in Montgomery, Alabama, and it concluded after King's death with an Epilogue that touched on events as different as the death of Lyndon Baines Johnson, the end of the Vietnam War, the dismantling of the Berlin Wall, and the release of Nelson Mandela from prison in South Africa. Branch felt that King had upheld to the end the doctrine of non-violence.

Sitkoff wrote that the books by Martin Luther King himself must be used with caution" because of his "ghostwriters." Although it is true that King relied on people like Bayard Rustin and Stanley Levison to help prepare his books, it is misleading to suggest that this somehow changed his message. One needs to read *Stride Toward Freedom* (1958) to understand firsthand the Montgomery bus boycott as well as his strategy of nonviolent action. *The Measure of a Man* (1959) included King's presentations at a national conference of the United Church of Christ. *Strength to Love* (1963) and *Trumpet of Conscience* (1967) brought together sermons preached by King at Dexter Avenue Church in Montgomery and Ebenezer Church in Atlanta, and repeated elsewhere around the country. *Why We Can't Wait* (1963) came out of the campaign in Alabama and included the famous "Letter from Birmingham Jail." *Where Do we Go From Here: Chaos or Community?* (1967) was his last book. In it he analyzed the "black power" slogan of Floyd McKissick and Stokely Carmichael, and showed both its strengths and weaknesses.

Three other recommended books were by his associates and contemporaries, Ralph David Abernathy, Andrew Young, and John Lewis. Although often in the shadow of Dr. King, Abernathy was a pioneer civil rights leader, who organized the Montgomery Improvement Association and persuaded King to be its president. Abernathy marched with King and went to jail with him. After the assassination he succeeded King as

4. Washington, *The Essential Writings and Speeches*, xx

president of the Southern Christian Leadership Conference. His autobiography was entitled *And the Walls Came Tumbling Down*, published in 1989. Young was on the staff of the National Council of Churches, with its headquarters in New York City, from 1957 to 1961, when he and his wife, Jean, decided they needed to return south to work in programs of citizenship education and voter registration. To support these programs an arrangement was made with the Field Foundation to send money through the United Church Board for Homeland Ministries, so that Young was on the UCC staff, but had his office in Atlanta next to Dr. King. Young became executive director of the SCLC in 1964 and later served as its executive vice president until 1970 when he ran for the U.S. Congress in Georgia's fifth district. His book was published in 1996 with the title, *An Easy Burden: The Civil Rights Movement and the Transformation of America*. A third book was by John Lewis, head of the Student Nonviolent Coordinating Committee and for many years Congressman from the Fifth District, Georgia. It was called *Walking with the Wind: A Memoir of the Movement*.

A Life Cut Too Short

Martin Luther King, Jr. was born on January 15, 1929, in Atlanta, Georgia. He skipped several grades in school and finished high school in 1944. Before entering college he went to Simsbury, Connecticut, to work in the tobacco fields, and appreciated the freedom to eat in restaurants and go to theatres without racial barriers. He graduated from Morehouse College in Atlanta in 1948 and Crozer Theological Seminary in Chester, Pennsylvania, in 1951, but he was ordained a minister on February 25, 1948. He was accepted for graduate study at Boston University and received the PhD degree in 1955. His dissertation was on "A Comparison of the Conception of God in the Thinking of Paul Tillich and Henry Nelson Wieman." King married Coretta Scott on June 18, 1953, in her home town of Marion, Alabama. The couple had four children, Yolanda, Martin III, Dexter, and Bernice.

In April 1954 he accepted the call to serve the Dexter Avenue Baptist Church in Montgomery, Alabama, and was installed on October 31. Over a year later, on December 1, 1955, Rosa Parks was arrested because she would not give up her seat on the bus when she was traveling home from her work. The bus boycott began on December 5, and King was elected president of the Montgomery Improvement Association. He had a profound religious experience in his kitchen the following month, on January

27, around midnight. After receiving many obscene and threatening phone calls and death threats, he could not sleep and was ready to give up. According to David Garrow he heard an inner voice, and Jesus told him, "Stand up for righteousness. Stand up for justice. Stand up for truth. And lo I will be with you, even unto the end of the world."[5] Three days later his house was bombed, but no one was hurt. King rushed home and confronted an angry crowd seeking retaliation. His philosophy of nonviolence was put to the test, but he calmed the crowd and sent them home. The boycott ended on December 21, 1956, when the U.S. Supreme Court declared the laws of bus segregation unconstitutional.

After several days of meetings in Atlanta the Southern Leaders Conference (later the Southern Christian Leadership Conference) was organized on February 14, 1957, by a group of African-American ministers, and King was chosen the president. The following month he and other Americans traveled to Ghana to celebrate the independence of that new nation, and this was followed by visits to several major cities in Europe. In May he delivered an address, "Give us the ballot," in Washington, DC, at the Prayer Pilgrimage for Freedom. Over Labor Day weekend King, along with Ralph Abernathy visited briefly the Highlander Folk School in Tennessee, since it was celebrating its twenty-fifth anniversary. Founded by Myles Horton, it was one place in the southern states where white and black leaders, especially labor organizers, could gather.

1958 was a difficult year; early in September King was arrested in Montgomery and jailed briefly, because he had gone down to the courthouse to support his friend, Ralph Abernathy. On September 20 he was stabbed in a Harlem department store while signing copies of his book, *Stride Toward Freedom*; he spent two weeks in the hospital and then several months recuperating at home. In February 1959 Martin and Coretta King, along with Lawrence Reddick, journeyed to India to visit associates of Gandhi and to have dinner with Prime Minister Nehru. On the way home they stopped in Jerusalem and Cairo.

During these years King not only faced the resistance and intransigence of the established powers in the South determined to preserve segregation and white supremacy, but also many African-Americans who did not want to get involved. Also, he experienced the rivalries and jealousies of the leaders of older organizations who resented his new prominence and prestige, such as Roy Wilkins of the NAACP, Whitney Young of the Urban

5. Garrow, *Bearing the Cross*, 58

League, and James Farmer of the Congress of Racial Equality. They had relied on tried-and-true methods of litigation and legislation and were wary of boycotts, marches, and demonstration. In addition the "sit-in" movement began on February 1, 1960, at the lunch counter of the Woolworth Store in Greensboro, North Carolina, and two months later the Student Nonviolent Coordinating Committee was organized.

The young SNCC leaders tended to be more militant and felt that King did not go far enough. Dr. King and the SCLC found themselves reacting and responding to movements, which they had not initiated, such as the "sit-ins," the "freedom-rides" of 1961, the Albany, Georgia, movement of 1961–62, the Mississippi "Freedom Summer," and the St. Augustine, Florida, movement of 1964. King was also confronted with problems of staffing and funding for the SCLC, and he suffered from exhaustion due to his grueling travel schedule and speaking engagements all over the country. According to Garrow, his telephones and hotel rooms were "bugged" by J. Edgar Hoover of the FBI, who accused King of Communist leanings and extra-marital relations. The wiretapping had been authorized by Attorney General Robert Kennedy, but Hoover went much further because he was determined to destroy King. It was learned later that there was also an FBI informant planted within the SCLC office in Atlanta.

The year 1963 stood out, because SCLC took the initiative to organize in Birmingham, Alabama, where the Police Commissioner was Eugene "Bull" Connor, who was determined to preserve segregation by all means. While in jail, King received a letter from white clergy asking him to end the demonstrations. On April 16 he wrote the "Letter From Birmingham Jail," which was one of his finest statements in support of nonviolent direct action. As President, John F. Kennedy announced in June that he was proposing major civil rights legislation, and King met with him at the White House. It was on August 28 that King delivered the final address at the March on Washington "For Jobs and Freedom" in front of the Lincoln Memorial to a crowd that numbered about 250,000 people. This became famous as the "I Have A Dream" speech. Eighteen days later a dynamite blast killed four little girls attending Sunday school at the Sixteenth Street Baptist Church in Birmingham. After Kennedy's assassination, Lyndon Johnson promised to follow through, and he signed the Civil Rights Act on July 2, 1964. King received the Nobel Peace Prize in Oslo, Norway, on December 10.

In 1965 the SCLC organized a movement in Selma, Alabama, which led to the "Bloody Sunday" march over the Edmund Pettus Bridge, and finally to the Selma to Montgomery march, concluding on March 25. By August the sweeping Voting Rights Act had been passed by large majorities in both houses of Congress. Dr. King turned his attention to northern and western cities in the country. The riots and racial violence in the Watts section of Los Angeles in August 1965 had demonstrated the deep frustration of African-Americans and others who were caught in ghettos that were created by housing, banking, and other restrictions. Among the cities he considered was Boston, where he addressed a joint session of the legislature on April 22 and spoke to a large crowd in the pouring rain on Boston Commons on April 23.

He chose the city of Chicago because it was one of the most segregated cities, but also because it had a strong Coordinating Council of Community Organizations. However, he also faced the dominant political machine of Mayor Richard Daley, and the results were disappointing, except for programs like Operation Breadbasket led by Jesse Jackson. In the middle of the year King reacted to another initiative, the planned "March Against Fear," by James Meredith, from the Tennessee state line to Jackson, Mississippi. Meredith was shot by a sniper on his first day, and King and other leaders rushed to his hospital bed in Memphis and vowed to continue the march. It was on this march that Stokely Carmichael of SNCC used the slogan "black power" for the first time.

For several years King had opposed the Vietnam War, but it was on April 4, 1967, that he gave a major speech on the subject at Riverside Church in New York City at a meeting of Clergy and Laity Concerned About Vietnam. He became one of the co-chairmen and worked with Dr. Benjamin Spock, William Sloane Coffin, and others. King's activity against the Vietnam War split members of the SCLC Board and brought opposition from other Civil Rights leaders, because they felt it would hurt the cause. It also infuriated Lyndon Johnson.

King's last major effort was the organization of the "Poor People's Campaign," which was intended to bring together African-Americans, Hispanics, Native Americans, and poor whites from Appalachia and elsewhere. A march on Washington and the building of a tent "Resurrection City" along the Mall were planned for May 1968, but King was deterred by an invitation to help in the strike of sanitation workers in Memphis, Tennessee. One march in Memphis was disrupted by violence, but King was determined to return and lead a second one. Before that could happen, he was killed by a sniper on April 4, 1968, while standing on the balcony of the Lorraine Motel, preparing to go out to dinner. He was only thirty-nine years old, and left a wife and four small children. The "Poor People's March" was held in June, but the encampment itself was plagued by rain, mud, and poor logistics, and the remaining demonstrators were evicted by the police.

Historians will debate his legacy for generations, but the consensus is that the country was completely transformed by his leadership. The marches and demonstrations had led to the most far-reaching civil rights legislation since the Civil War and Reconstruction. Segregated buses and other facilities had been declared unconstitutional. The Voting Rights Act had removed barriers to voter registration and had provided monitors for voting districts. The war against poverty had become a part of the national agenda, until it was undermined by another war in Southeast Asia. Much had been accomplished, but much more needed to be done. Like Moses on Mt. Nebo looking out over Canaan, as recorded in the Book of Deuter-onomy in the Bible, King felt that he had been to the mountaintop and had seen the promised land, but he was not going to get there.

Corrections and Additions to the Historical Record

King and Yale University

There has been some disagreement about Dr. King and his intentions for graduate study. In Volume I of the King papers, compiled by Clayborne Carson, there is a copy of a letter written by King in January 1951 to Sankey Lee Blanton, president of Crozer Theological Seminary. King wrote that he had already been accepted by Edinburgh University, Scotland, and Boston University, but not by Yale because he had not yet taken the Graduate Re-cord Examination. He indicated that Yale was his preference. Furthermore, in the same volume is a copy of his scores on the GRE as of March 6, 1951, which showed that he scored high in Literature but in a low percentile in other subjects. Yale did not accept him, so he went to Boston University.

The King papers also showed that he was invited by the undergraduate lecture bureau to give a major address in Woolsey Hall at Yale on January 14, 1959. His subject was "The Future of Integration," which was published in the Yale alumni magazine and elsewhere. Before the lecture he had a private meeting with Yale's president, Whitney Griswold, and that evening there was a bomb threat, although no bomb was found. A surprise birthday party was thrown for him at the residential Pierson College. The next day he spoke in Marquand Chapel at Yale Divinity School on "Problems of the South."

At the invitation of Yale's chaplain, William Sloane Coffin, he preached at Battell Chapel in January 1962, and after Kingman Brewster became president, Yale awarded him the honorary degree of LLD on June 15, 1964. The story was told that King had been released from jail in St. Augustine in time to travel to New Haven.

Mississippi Summer Project of 1964

Writers have not been accurate about the Mississippi summer project. Attention has been paid to the hundreds of student volunteers, primarily white, who came to Mississippi to work on a project, originally planned by SNCC, which included freedom schools, citizenship education, and voter registration. The book by John Lewis was one of the few that recognized the presence of several hundred clergy, lawyers, doctors, and medical personnel. Many clergy were enlisted by the National Council of Churches, which had provided the funds for the training sessions in Ohio and at Tougaloo College in Jackson, Mississippi. The National Council developed special programs in Hattiesburg and Canton.

The *Minneapolis Star-Tribune* interviewed Rabbi Jerome Ludnick of Adath Jeshurun synagogue and myself from the Mayflower Community Congregational Church after we both returned from Mississippi in August. Rabbi Ludnick commented on the disappearance of three civil rights workers (who were later found dead and buried in an earthen dam in Philadelphia, Mississippi). I said that people in Mississippi refer to two periods of time, "Before Philadelphia" and "After Philadelphia," and that the burning of churches and the continual harassment of workers hasn't stopped, but the deaths have.

Although "Freedom Summer" was initiated by SNCC, it is important to remember that the SCLC, NAACP, and CORE collaborated in what was called the Council of Federated Organizations. King himself visited the state and spoke in four communities, Greenwood, Meridian, Vicksburg, and Jackson. The climax of the summer was the creation of the Mississippi Freedom Democratic Party, which went to the national Democratic Party convention in Atlantic City to challenge the all-white delegation. King had supported the final compromise which was worked out by Senator Hubert Humphrey and his protégé, Walter Mondale, the attorney general of

Minnesota, but it was rejected by MFDP delegates. However, it meant that future conventions would seat fairly elected delegations.

Freedom Songs

The Civil Rights movement was fueled by freedom songs. Of all the writers, Andrew Young has done the best job in capturing the spirit and enthusiasm of these songs, some of which grew out of spirituals and labor songs; others were adapted from gospel songs, and others emerged spontaneously from the marchers and demonstrators, who no longer feared jail and would not be intimidated. Young devoted a chapter in his book, *An Easy Burden*, to "The Singing Movement." The Albany, Georgia, movement may have been disappointing, but out of it came a repertoire of such songs. Young took a break from his work in November 1964 and came to Minneapolis, preached at two services at Mayflower Church, spoke at a large youth rally, and led hundreds of Minnesota young people in singing freedom songs.

It is claimed that "We Shall Overcome," the anthem of the Civil Rights movement, was adapted from a gospel hymn written around 1901 by Charles A. Tindley (1851–1933), pastor of a large African Methodist Episcopal Church in Philadelphia, now known as "Tindley Temple." One of his many hymns was called "I'll overcome someday," but it had a different melody. His words were sung to a different tune from an antebellum spiritual, "No more auction block for me," and brought to Highlander Folk School in the 1930s by tobacco workers from Charlestown, South Carolina. Zilphia Horton, wife of the founder of the school, was the song leader and picked it up. Pete Seeger, a folksinger in the tradition of Woody Guthrie, changed the words to "We shall overcome." According to Andrew Young, Dr. King heard the song at Highlander in 1957 and spoke approvingly of it in a car trip from Highlander to an engagement in Louisville, Kentucky.

Women in the Civil Rights Movement

The death of Dorothy Height in 2010 was a reminder of the important role of women in the Civil Rights movement. She was a YWCA executive and president of the National Council of Negro Women for forty years. Her work for equality and justice went back to the anti-lynching protests of the 1930s and the integration of YWCA facilities in the 1940s. Although she received several of the country's highest honors, she remained in the shadow of the men who led the SCLC, the NAACP, SNCC, and CORE. The only mention of her in David Garrow's biography of King was her meeting with President Kennedy in 1961, along with the other leaders. At the March on Washington in 1963 she had an honored place on the platform, an arm's length from Dr. King, but she was not invited to speak. Any list of women leaders in the movement would be long, but it would certainly include Rosa Parks, who inspired the Montgomery bus boycott, Jo Ann Robinson, Septima Clark, Ella Baker, Fannie Lou Hamer of the Mississippi Freedom Democratic Party, Diane Nash, and the wives of King and Abernathy, Coretta Scott and Juanita.

The Declaration of Independence and the U.S. Constitution

Dr. King often appealed to the founding documents of the country. In his "Letter From Birmingham Jail" he cited the words of Thomas Jefferson in the Declaration of Independence, "we hold these truths to be self-evident, that all men are created equal." In his "I have a dream" speech King maintained that the country's founders had signed a "promissory note," but America had defaulted and African-Americans were left empty-handed. His concept of the "American dream" was the unfulfilled vision of people of all races, creeds, and nationalities living together as sisters and brothers.

It should not be forgotten that King also appealed to the First Amendment of the Constitution, namely "the right of the people peaceably to assemble, and to petition the Government for a redress of grievances." He took this right seriously and literally, which was why King organized peaceful and nonviolent assemblies in churches and elsewhere, followed by marches to courthouses, state capitols and Washington, DC, to petition for a redress of grievances. These grievances were many, not the least of which was the denial of the right to vote. They were beaten or fired from their jobs when they registered or voted, and in some southern counties there was not a single African-American voter. The Fifteenth Amendment stated: "The right of the citizens of the United States to vote shall not be denied or abridged by the United States or by any State on account of race, color or previous condition of servitude." King lamented the fact that they had to work so hard, suffer, and die for something that was rightfully theirs. King also appreciated the Constitution's independent judiciary, which served as a check and balance on other branches of government. Some of the greatest gains of the movement came from the decisions of the federal courts and the U.S. Supreme Court.

Conclusion

It would come as no surprise to say how important religious faith was in the life of Martin Luther King, Jr. As he indicated himself, he grew up in the African-American church, and his father and a grandfather were Baptist ministers. He was ordained a minister at an early age, graduated from a theological seminary, and studied theology at Boston University. Yet, his lineage and education are not sufficient in themselves to explain his deep trust in God's action in history in the face of beatings, arrests, jailing, a near death experience by stabbing, mob hostility, death threats, not to mention the organized opposition of governors, mayors, police chiefs, sheriffs, the White Citizens Council, and the Ku Klux Klan. Part of his dedication and determination to go on can be traced to his profound religious experience in his kitchen in January 1956. However, there was his inner belief that God ruled the world, that his Kingdom of love, peace, and righteousness was coming.

King adapted a quote from Theodore Parker, Unitarian minister and abolitionist in Boston: "The arc of the moral universe is a long one, but it bends toward justice." Despite all the setbacks, King was convinced that God was working his purpose out.

King had a faith that could move mountains. It was grounded in the God of the Bible, who brought forth the Israelites from Egyptian bondage, across the sea and the wilderness, into the promised land. It was a God who heard his people cry, who listened to their murmurings, their spiritual songs in slavery, who raised up leaders to organize rebellions, to shepherd them to freedom, to emancipate them, to remove the shackles of ignorance and oppression. It was this God who worked through King and his associates and the thousands of folk who were not going to take it anymore, who were not going to be turned around, who would keep on walking and talking.

Biographers have been right to remind us of King's humanity, that he was not a saint, and this gave mere mortals more courage. The commentators have been right to tell us that we have forgotten how radical King was, in calling for re-structuring society, for the re-distribution of economic and political power. Vincent Harding was right in saying that we prefer the sunshine of King's "I Have A Dream" speech over the shadows of his years of opposition to the Vietnam War, his identification with the poor, his work with the sanitation workers. The poet was right, that it is easier to build monuments than to make a better world. It is easier to declare a holiday, a day off from school or work, than it is to transform all days, all schools, all work.

How shall we observe Martin Luther King, Jr. Day? By recalling his humanity, by restoring his image, by renewing his struggle against evil, by recalling the chartered freedoms of our country's founding documents, by re-invigorating all Americans (it is not a day just for government officials and African-Americans to observe), by singing the freedom songs, by re-claiming his message, by reciting the mighty deeds of a God who is active in history. Dr. King asked that he be remembered as a drum major for justice, righteousness, and truth. If he was the drum major, where are the human instruments to carry on his work: to make poverty a thing of the past; to remove the scourge of war; to take down the barriers that separate people of different races, creeds, and nations; to lift the burden of materialism that stifles the human spirit? Much was accomplished by King and the Civil Rights movement to redeem the soul of America; much more needs to be done.

When Rabbi Abraham Joshua Heschel introduced King ten days be-fore he was assassinated to the annual convention of the Rabbinical As-sembly, he asked, "Where are the prophets of Israel today?" and referred to King as a modern prophet to America. Heschel urged his listeners to heed King's voice and vision. "The whole future of America will depend upon the impact and influence of Dr. King."[6]

6. Oates, *Let the Trumpet Sound,* 473

CHAPTER 2

First in the Hearts of His Countrymen

WASHINGTON'S BIRTHDAY, PRESIDENT'S DAY

IN HIS EULOGY AFTER the death of George Washington, Gen. Henry ("Light Horse Harry") Lee uttered the familiar words, "First in war, first in peace, first in the hearts of his countrymen." Lee had expressed what was generally felt, that this was the end of an era, that the death of the first U.S. President marked the end of the life of the person who, more than any other, had led the country to independence from Great Britain, had governed the new nation in its early years, and had endeared himself to the American people. Yet, at the end of the twentieth century Richard Brookhiser would write about Washington: that he is in our textbooks and our wallets, but not in our hearts. It is true that most people with pocketbooks or wallets carry artistic representations of Washington, the Gilbert Stuart portrait on the one-dollar bill and the bust from the statue created by the French sculptor, Jean-Antoine Houdon, on the quarter, but the first President seems distant and cold, a monument rather than a man, a marble statue rather than flesh and blood. For some people he even seems dull!

People do not have the affection for him today that was prevalent during his life, because it seems like ancient history when a young surveyor became a colonel in the Virginia militia in the French and Indian War, was elected a delegate to the Continental Congress, became Commander in Chief of the army, and then presided over the Constitutional Convention, and was elected the first U.S. President. He seems very distant, also, because he represented a way of life in the southern states that was ended by the Civil War. Despite his leadership in the struggle for freedom and a republican form of government, Washington was a part of the landed gentry and planter aristocracy that relied on slavery to be economically viable and competitive.

However, even in his lifetime Washington seemed aloof and distant. His personality was very formal and reserved, because he kept tight control over his feelings and especially his temper. He did not like to shake hands with strangers and be touched. It was reported that his face rarely showed any emotion, and it didn't help to have uncomfortable dentures, making it difficult to smile. In religious matters, many scholars have labeled him a deist, or at the very most a lukewarm Anglican who was uncomfortable with more evangelical expressions of faith. One would hope that much could be learned from his voluminous correspondence, especially from his letters to his wife when they were separated for long periods of time but, unfortunately, Martha burned nearly all them when he died, making it impossible for us to replicate a volume such as the "Dearest Friend" correspondence of John and Abigail Adams.

However, the people of his day expressed great love and affection for him. His soldiers and officers admired his bravery and resolution. One of the great moments at the end of the Revolutionary War occurred when his officers met at Newburgh, New York, to plan an insurrection because they had not received their pay and benefits. Washington appeared in their midst to address them and moved them to tears when he spoke of his graying hair and failing eyesight because of his long years of sacrifice for his country, thus averting any trouble. The people loved him. On his trip to New York City for his first inauguration throngs gathered along the way, putting up triumphal arches and bestowing laurel wreaths and flowers. Band music and people on horseback escorted him into towns. At dinners and balls, people wanted to be near him and ladies wanted to dance with him. Parents wanted to name their babies after him. Even in final retirement his beloved Mount Vernon became a stagecoach stop on the way to Alexandria, as people came to see him unannounced and often stayed for dinner and even overnight! He was bombarded with requests from artists and a sculptor (who stayed at Mount Vernon for about a week) to pose for posterity, and copies of his likeness were in great demand. Washington was a military hero, a celebrity, the symbol of a united country, a national icon, and a part of the American pantheon.

Washington was what biographer James Thomas Flexner called "The Indispensable Man." He was twice elected unanimously as the U.S.

President, the only person to hold that distinction. Indeed, the delegates at the Constitutional Convention in Philadelphia in 1787 had only Washington in mind when they drafted the article on the executive branch; the only question was whether anyone else could fill his shoes. Washington could have occupied the office for life, but chose to step down after two terms to return to what he called his "vine and fig tree" at Mount Vernon. In those eight years in office he kept the country out of war and established precedents that have guided it ever since. The new federal district was named after him, and he helped lay the cornerstone of the Capitol building, wearing his Masonic regalia. (Nobody knows where the cornerstone is today!)

Biographer Joseph J. Ellis has pointed out that Washington's Birthday became a national holiday the first year of his presidency. Long before it ever became a federal holiday it was celebrated in many ways throughout the country. On the centennial of his birth in 1832, the U.S. Congress adjourned for the day in his honor, and the following year a Washington National Monument Society was formed to erect a suitable memorial. The Washington Monument was built in two stages, from 1848 to 1856, and from 1876 to 1884, because of a lack of funds and the interruption of the Civil War. The monument was dedicated in 1885.

In the meantime a federal holiday recognizing his birthday began in 1880 and was expanded in 1885 to include all government workers in the District of Columbia and the rest of the country. As the first holiday to honor an American, it was widely observed by many organizations, clubs, churches and synagogues, schools, colleges, towns, and states. On the 200th anniversary of Washington's birth my wife's grandfather wrote a poem honoring Washington for a program at the Grange in Middletown, Connecticut. Temperance organizations throughout the country were named for him. In 1968 the holiday was established on the third Monday of February, which meant that his birthday would never be celebrated on the day he was born! This federal holiday has been called Presidents' Day, which gave the false impression that it was also honoring Lincoln or all Presidents. (See *Appendix A, Lincoln's Birthday*.)

When he died in 1799 the entire country went into mourning. In addition to eulogies and services, there were many engraved tributes to him, and even pictorial works in embroidery, using common symbols of grief and immortality. Most striking was a series of engravings called the "Apotheosis of George Washington," which seemed to glorify and even deify him. It is reported that one artist, Rembrandt Peale, created an early sample and that it was revised and reproduced by David Edwin in 1800. The engraving showed Washington ascending into heaven from Mt. Vernon, guided by a winged cherub and welcomed by Generals Richard Montgomery and Joseph Warren, who were both killed in early battles of the Revolutionary War. The original is in the National Portrait Gallery of the Smithsonian, along with a similar scene on a ceramic pitcher! The most famous "Apotheosis" was painted in 1865 in the fresco style on the ceiling of the U.S. Capitol canopy, 180 feet over the rotunda, by the Italian artist, Constantino Brumidi. In the center of the scene Washington is depicted rising into heaven in glory, escorted by female figures representing Liberty and Victory. Six groups of figures are on the perimeter of the scene, representing War, Science, Marine, Commerce, Mechanics, and Agriculture.

A Very Human Icon

Washington had somewhat of an aristocratic family background, yet he led the country to a more classless republic. An ancestor was a graduate of Oxford University and served in various capacities as an Anglican cleric. One can still visit the ancestral home at Sulgrave Manor, not far from Banbury in Oxfordshire, England. His great grandfather, John, settled in Virginia in 1656 and began the tradition of acquiring land. His father, Augustine, and his first wife had two sons and a daughter. After his wife died, Augustine married Mary Ball and they had six children, George being the oldest. He was born on February 11, 1732, at Pope's Creek in Westmoreland County, not far from the Potomac River. (When the new Gregorian calendar was adopted, his birth date was changed to February 22.) The family moved twice, to Hunting Creek on the Potomac (later renamed Mount Vernon), and then to Ferry Farm, which was located across the Rappahannock River from the town of Fredericksburg.

Of all his siblings, Washington was closest to his older half-brother, Lawrence, who had fought in the West Indies under British Admiral Edward Vernon. Lawrence inherited the Hunting Creek farm and named it Mount Vernon in honor of the Admiral. Washington's only trip outside the American mainland was to Barbados with Lawrence, who was hoping that the change in climate might improve his health. The future general and U.S. President developed smallpox on the island, which immunized him from the disease when it later ran rampant through army encampments. After Lawrence and his heirs died, Washington acquired Mount Vernon and through the years made many improvements and additions to the property using architectural skills.

Washington had a very difficult relationship with his mother. According to biographer Ron Chernow, she was stubborn and self-centered. Even though Mary Ball Washington lived long enough to see her son elected as the first President of the United States, she did not acknowledge or appreciate his accomplishments. She lived comfortably at Ferry Farm and later in Fredericksburg, but she felt that she wasn't cared for by her son, and she even applied for financial assistance from the Commonwealth of Virginia. It is clear that Washington did not want his mother to live at Mount Vernon. He did not have any children of his own, but helped to raise Martha's two children as well as step-grandchildren, and other relatives.

The education that Washington received was limited, and he regretted throughout his life that he had not attended college. The hope was that he would go back to England and study at Appleby Grammar School like his two half-brothers, but his father's death when young Washington was eleven years old made that impossible. Instead, he went to schools at Fredericksburg and elsewhere, and had a tutor, but the most important thing he learned was the art and science of surveying. This opened up a whole new world for him, as he travelled to the Shenandoah, the Alleghenies, and the wilderness beyond. However, his lack of a more extensive education did not prevent him from being a voracious reader and an avid correspondent.

Much has been made of Washington's copying of a set of maxims from *The Rules of Civility and Decent Behavior in Company and Conversation*, a sixteenth century Jesuit production in France. This work may have shaped a personality that was polite, correct, and reserved, but it did not keep him at an early age from enjoying such pastimes as card-playing, cockfighting, horse-racing, and fox-hunting. He learned dancing, fencing, and horsemanship. He enjoyed the theatre, convivial dinners with wine, and fashionable clothes. His life was very orderly, and he worked very hard to maintain his reputation and an image of integrity and punctuality.

Washington lived beyond his means. Actually, he was land-rich and cash poor through much of his life. He bought thousands of acres of land, but was not always able to sell them at a profit, and he had trouble with people occupying the tracts and not paying the rent. He seemed to be always in debt to a London agent who sold his tobacco abroad, and purchased luxurious goods for Mount Vernon. It was reported that Washington had to borrow the money in order to travel to New York City for his first inauguration as President. However, it needs to be pointed out that he never received a salary for his services with the Continental Army, and as President, he was reimbursed only for expenses.

Long before the term was invented, Washington was an agribusinessman. He added four farms to his Mount Vernon estate and would daily travel by horseback to inspect them. He experimented with crop rotation, added corn, wheat, oats, and barley to take the place of tobacco, which depleted the soil, and he pioneered in the breeding of mules. When he was away, his correspondence was filled with detailed instructions to his overseers about farming. He was up-to-date on the latest agricultural developments, including a new kind of plow and thresher. On his property were a greenhouse, gristmill, fishery, distillery, and a blacksmith shop.

He was committed to the development of an infrastructure for the American colonies and new nation. More than any other person, because of his extensive travel, he was concerned about the condition of roads and the lack of bridges. Washington was convinced that the Potomac River could be opened up for navigation to the western lands, partly to bind these new settlers to the eastern seacoast. He became president of the Potomac River Company and sought the advice of experts on the building of locks and canals.

Washington was a ladies man. Before he married Martha, he fell in love with the wife of his best friend and neighbor, Sally Fairfax, who lived with her husband George William Fairfax at a plantation near Mount Vernon called Belvoir. Years later Sally and her husband moved to England. Washington wrote to Sally in the last years of his life, expressing the view that his visits with her at Belvoir were "happy moments—the happiest of my life—which I have enjoyed in your company."[1] While in Philadelphia as President, Washington developed a close relationship with Eliza Powell, the wife of the mayor, a very knowledgeable and sophisticated lady. Scholars have pointed out that it was Eliza's letter to the President at the end of his first term which convinced him to run for a second term rather than to retire to Mount Vernon. At many functions in the seat of government and elsewhere in the country Washington would keep track of the number of women in attendance and would comment on their being "handsome."

For a man of imposing strength and stamina, Washington seemed to suffer from a number of ailments. Besides smallpox as a youth, he had bouts of malaria, dysentery, fever and a respiratory illness. In the early years

---

1. Chernow, *Washington: A Life*, 778

of the Revolutionary War he was laid low for ten days. In early 1787, prior to the Constitutional Convention in Philadelphia, he had his arm in a sling because of rheumatic pain. In the first two years of his presidency he had a tumor twice removed from his thigh and was bed-ridden for days. People feared that he was going to die, and the President himself was mindful of the shortened lives of the males in his family. In addition, he had failing eyesight, and hearing and dental problems.

He inherited slaves and was a slaveholder throughout his life. Any reservations that he had about the practice seemed to stem from its cost effectiveness, rather than from any principle of morality. He may have been the only one of the slaveholding founders to liberate them at his death, but in his life he used various stratagems to keep them in his control. Recent excavations of the executive mansion in Philadelphia have revealed more of the details of his nine household slaves, and a modern exhibit shows their condition of servitude, incongruously situated right next to the Liberty Bell pavilion. He used some deception to keep them from being freed in a state like Pennsylvania; he even used a customs official to track down one woman, Oney Judge, who had escaped to live in New Hampshire, and he also tried to recover a cook named Hercules. The Washingtons seemed to be oblivious to the fervent desire of African-Americans to be free. There is one oral tradition that said Washington fathered a child with a slave from another plantation, but historians including Ron Chernow have dismissed it.

A Man for All Stations

Washington wrote that his whole life had been dedicated to the service of his country in one way or another. For over forty years Washington was involved in the life and leadership of the emerging new nation. In the nineteenth century Daniel Webster, Henry Clay, and John C. Calhoun each served for about forty years in positions of national leadership, but none of them became President. Washington served in the French and Indian War, led the Continental Army that won independence, presided over the framing of the Constitution, and then was elected the country's first President. No other person in American history has contributed in so many ways. In addition, he was a member of Virginia's House of Burgesses, served as a vestryman at two Anglican parishes, was elected to the Continental Congress, and organized the Potomac River Company.

Washington tried again and again to secure an officer's commission with the British military, but was unsuccessful. What he did achieve was leadership in the Virginia militia, and he was second-in-command to General Braddock at the time of the French and Indian War. Historians are generally agreed that Washington's trip to the "Forks of the Ohio" (present-day Pittsburgh) and western Pennsylvania and the killing of a French envoy were the sparks that lit the conflagration. He learned from his mistakes and on the disastrous Braddock venture showed bravery and skill under fire. Historian Fred Anderson has called the French and Indian War "the war that made America." Before the war the colonists were bottled up on the eastern seaboard; after the war they expanded to the Great Lakes and the Ohio and Mississippi River valleys. Prior to the conflict they were separated and competing with each other; afterwards, they moved toward cooperation and unity. Also, the colonists lacked a sense of self-esteem before the war and were treated like inferiors and second-class citizens by the British; afterwards, the war changed that and gave them a new sense of confidence.

It was the Lexington and Concord alarms and the battle of Bunker Hill (which actually occurred on Breed's Hill) which galvanized the Continental Congress into action. Washington appeared at the Congress attired in his militia uniform and was unanimously elected to command the American forces. Much has been written about the Revolutionary War: the evacuation of Boston by the British; the few successes in battle; the terrible winter at Valley Forge; the lack of food, clothing, and supplies for the soldiers; the intrigues and attempts to replace Washington; the victory at Saratoga and the French alliance; the treachery of Benedict Arnold; the British occupations of Philadelphia and New York City; the victory at Yorktown. Washington emerged from the war as a military hero and the most popular man in America.

He was "present at the creation" of the country and lent his name and prestige to the undertaking. His war experience convinced Washington of the need for a strong, central, "energetic" government which could levy taxes, recruit and supply an army, make treaties, regulate money and commerce. He invited representatives of Maryland and Virginia to Mount Vernon to resolve navigation disputes on the Potomac River. This led to a conference at Annapolis, which was only attended by delegates from five states, and finally a convention in Philadelphia in 1787 to revise the Articles of Confederation, which were not working. Washington was a member of the Virginia delegation and was unanimously elected the presiding officer, giving instant credibility to the enterprise. His support of the proposed new Constitution almost guaranteed that it would be adopted.

Although he was not a delegate to his state's ratifying convention, he was not a disinterested bystander, but an active advocate, an enthusiastic cheerleader and a tireless networker. Cokie Roberts in her book, *Founding Mothers: The Women Who Raised Our Nation*, referred to Washington at his "command post at Mount Vernon," managing a constant flow of news and correspondence on the progress of ratifying the new framework for government.

More recent historians have re-appraised the tenure of the first U.S. President and have found it both effective and trend-setting. Washington succeeded in adding flesh to the skeleton of the Constitution, in putting into practice what was conceived in theory. He established important precedents in relationships with Cabinet members, Congress, the judiciary, diplomats, and other countries. He was wise in supporting Hamilton's plans to place the country on a firm financial foundation. He was responsible for selecting the site of the new federal district after a compromise was arrived at by the Congress, paying the debts of the northeastern states and placing the national capital in the southern states.

Washington decried the emerging parties of those favoring British or French interests and insisted on placing American interests first. He was the only President in the history of the country to put on his military uniform and lead a force, when he was called on to quell the "whiskey rebellion" in western Pennsylvania. Most important, he retired from the office after two terms and oversaw the peaceful transition to a new administration under John Adams. Even in retirement he was asked to be the Commander of an army if war were to break out between the new nation and France. Fortunately, war was averted.

Many Biographies of Washington

Washington never wrote the story of his life. The closest thing we have to an autobiography are the notes that he appended to a manuscript by David Humphreys, a military aide, whom he had recruited to write his biography. This was never published. An early biography that did come off the presses was one by Mason Locke Weems ("Parson Weems"), an itinerant preacher and book-seller, entitled *The Life of George Washington with Curious Anecdotes Equally Honorable to Himself and Exemplary to His Young*

Countrymen. This book became very popular and went through many editions. Abraham Lincoln read it in his boyhood. In the sixth edition Weems introduced the famous story of the chopping down of the cherry tree, which historians have called pure fiction.

Some of the great names in American life and literature have tried their hand at the story of Washington's life. John Marshall, the longest-serving Chief Justice of the U.S. Supreme Court, wrote *The Life of George Washington* in five volumes in 1804–1807. Toward the end of his life Washington Irving, one of the babies named after the President, wrote another five-volume biography, *The Life of George Washington*, in the years 1855–1859. Along with another biographer, Irving reported for the first time that in his inaugural oath Washington had added the words, "so help me God," even though it has never been supported by other sources, and participants in the ceremony could not hear the President because he spoke so softly. Woodrow Wilson, the future President, wrote a biography in 1897.

The twentieth century saw the publication of two monumental works about Washington. One was by Douglas Southall Freeman, a journalist and historian, who had been editor of *The Richmond News Leader* for many years. Entitled *George Washington: A Biography*, it was published in seven volumes between 1948 and 1957. The second was the four-volume biography by James Thomas Flexner, who had also started as a journalist but then concentrated on the writing of history and biography. Flexner condensed his four volumes into one volume, *Washington: The Indispensable Man*, which was published in 1974. A new paperback edition was published in 1984 to go along with the production of two TV mini-series on his life produced by MGM and broadcast by CBS, with Barry Bostwick playing the part of Washington. Both of the TV programs were based on Flexner's work, and he served as a consultant on the project.

In the twenty-first century there were additional books: *An Imperfect God: George Washington, His Slaves, and the Creation of America* by Henry Wiencek; *His Excellency: George Washington* by Joseph J. Ellis; and *The Ascent of George Washington: The Hidden Political Genius of an American Icon* by John Ferling. A prize-winning author, Ron Chernow, has quoted extensively from the letters and diaries of Washington, as well as other records, and has revealed a more complete human being in his 2010 volume, *Washington: A Life.* His goal was "to create a fresh portrait of Washington that will make him real, credible, and charismatic in the same way that he was perceived by his contemporaries."[2]

There is no end to Washington studies because of the extent of his correspondence, diaries, notes, reports, as well as letters to him. Washington himself was responsible for the preservation of his papers. Even during the Revolutionary War he hired secretaries to write and copy his many letters, and he went to great lengths to make sure that they were saved and archived at Mount Vernon.

Joining with the University of Virginia in the latest project on the papers of Washington is the Mount Vernon Ladies Association, the oldest national organization in the country devoted to historical preservation. This organization took over the ownership and management of Washington's beloved estate in 1860 and continues to unearth new materials and insights about his life. The Association was begun in 1853 by Ann Pamela Cunningham with the purpose of acquiring and restoring Washington's home. Since the Association was unable to get grants from any government agency, the women did their own fund-raising, with the help of the orator Edward Everett, who donated his lecture fees to the cause. Today the Association maintains about 500 acres, including fifty acres of gardens, a museum and education center, the tombs of George and Martha Washington, a greenhouse and agricultural exhibit, and a major collection of artifacts and manuscripts.

Washington and Religion

One of the most controversial issues of Washington's life has been his religion. The traditional view was that he was a Deist, accepting the scientific and rational sources of knowledge, not the revelations of Holy Writ, and looking upon God as a kind of watchmaker who wound up the world and then retired to let it tick away, not a deity who acts in human history. Freeman wrote that Washington had "no compelling faith in God," had no creedal set of beliefs and did not quote the Bible or the Prayer Book. Flexner concluded that he was a child of the Enlightenment, and that he was "like Benjamin Franklin and Thomas Jefferson, a deist." Flexner even added a footnote: "The reader should be warned that the forgers and myth-makers

2. Ibid, xx

have been endlessly active in their efforts to attribute to Washington their own religious acts and beliefs."[3]

A detailed study was published in 1963, *George Washington and Religion*, by Paul F. Boller, Jr., professor at Texas Christian University. Boller quoted Washington to say: "in politics, as in religion, my tenets are few and simple." The author referred to the paucity of biblical quotations in Washington's writings, the lack of references to the Christian religion, and the one allusion to Jesus in an address to the Delaware chiefs in 1779. Because Washington made no statements of Christian doctrine and did not participate in Holy Communion, Boller wondered whether he could be considered a Christian "except in the most nominal sense." The author concluded that "broadly speaking, of course, Washington can be classified as a Deist."[4]

In the first years of the twenty-first century there have been five studies which sought to present Washington as a mainstream Anglican and even a devout Christian and churchman. One of the most helpful was *Washington's God: Religion, Liberty, and the Father of Our Country*, published in 2006 and written by Michael Novak of the American Enterprise Institute and his daughter, Jana, a journalist and legislative aide. Another was *In the Hands of a Good Providence: Religion in the Life of George Washington*, which was written by Mary V. Thompson, research historian at the Mount Vernon Ladies Association, and published in 2008. It was no coincidence that the two volumes complement each other, since the Novaks saw the Thompson manuscript before it was published.

The Novaks were asked to write about Washington's religion by James Rees, executive director of Mount Vernon, because so many visitors inquired about the subject. What resulted from their "detective work" was the picture of a man of great integrity whose public and private life were seamless. In answer to the question whether Washington was a deist, the answer was negative; he was a mainstream Anglican. As to his use of the term "Providence," the Novaks found it based on the biblical tradition of a God who is active in history. As to whether Washington used religion for social and political purposes, the answer was again negative.

Mary V. Thompson made a major contribution to the conversation by her research into the religious traditions of the Washington family, both his generation and those that preceded and followed him. She has also dealt with his work on the Religion Committee of the Virginia House of

3. Flexner, *George Washington*, 245.
4. Boller, *George Washington and Religion*, 92, 93

Burgesses, his extensive library of books on religion and philosophy, and his benevolent and charitable works. She is one of the few scholars who acknowledged a kind of "latitudinarian" Anglican tradition, prevalent in the eighteenth century and especially in the southern states. She pointed out that this broad and tolerant faith was influenced by Arminianism (named after the Dutch theologian Jacobus Arminius). She has also called for further research on Washington's library, his involvement in the Masonic order (the tall Washington Masonic National Memorial in Alexandria, Virginia, was dedicated in 1932), and in the lives of later generations of the Washington-Custis families. Thompson has also reminded us that it is beyond human ability to judge whether a person is a Christian or not.

Frank E. Grizzard, Jr., who has worked with the papers of Washington and of the Lee family of Virginia, has prepared a slim volume, *The Ways of Providence: Religion and George Washington*, published in 2005. He has incorporated sections from his larger book on Washington and material on Washington's prayers by William Herbert Burk. Grizzard pointed out that the story of Washington praying at Valley Forge was first told in the seventeenth edition of Parson Weems's biography in 1817, and it "became and remains a central part of the lore surrounding Washington's religious life."[5]

A much larger book, *George Washington's Sacred Fire,* was published in 2006, written by Peter A. Lillback, president of Westminster Theological Seminary and pastor of the Proclamation Presbyterian Church in Bryn Mawr, Pennsylvania. It was an exhaustive treatment of Washington's writings and portrayed him as a very devout, orthodox Christian. Lillback even gave credence to the legends concocted by Weems. Finally, a 2004 book by Janice T. Connell, *Faith of Our Founding Father: The Spiritual Journey of George Washington*, has erroneously identified his ancestors as Anglican Catholics and has repeated the unsupported legend that Washington received Last Rites from the Roman Catholic Church before his death.

In the interest of full disclosure, Washington did attend church at least once a month while living in Virginia, according to his diaries, and much more often when he was President and visiting other parts of the country. Indeed, there could be signs in many places, "Washington worshipped here!" He was a communicant early in life, but with the severance of ties with Great Britain he often left the church service before Communion. Both his private and public writings have religious and biblical references. His use of the term "Providence" for a personal God was consistent with the

---

5. Grizzard, *The Ways of Providence*, 24

entire history of Christian doctrine, from the Patristics through Augustine, and Thomas Aquinas to John Calvin and the Puritans. It should not be confused with fate or destiny.

Separation of Church and State

Another controversial issue has been the concept of "separation of church and state." Tara Ross and Joseph C. Smith, Jr., two attorneys in Texas and Colorado respectively, have explored this subject in *Under God: George Washington and the Question of Church and State*, published in 2008. What the authors sought was to show that there was no such thing as separation between church and state for Washington, unlike Thomas Jefferson who wrote about a "wall of separation." What they succeeded in doing was to present Washington as the prime mover and shaker of what has been called "American civil religion," or the place of religion in American public life and history. The concept of "civil religion" did not appear in their work, but they use equivalent terms, such as "public religion," "official religion," "public piety," and the "role of religion in public life."

Ross and Smith show that Washington found ways to accommodate religion and government and to encourage and promote religion in the public realm. The authors have examined his military orders, correspondence, speeches, and proclamations, and have included many of these documents in their book. In his long career in public life Washington supported chaplains in the armed forces and in the Congress, issued proclamations calling for public prayer and thanksgiving, and supported tax funds to pay missionaries to convert and pacify Native American tribes. In his farewell address after two terms as President, Washington said that religion was essential for morality and good self-government.

In his first Thanksgiving proclamation in 1789 he recommended and assigned a day

> "to be devoted by the People of these States to the service of that great and glorious Being, whom is the beneficent Author of all the good that was, that is, or that will be—That we may then all unite in rendering unto him our sincere and humble thanks—for the peaceable and rational manner, in which we have been enabled to establish constitutions of government for our safety and happiness,

and particularly the national One now lately instituted—for the civil and religious liberty with which we are blessed . . . "[6]

The book, *Under God*, emphasized the adoption of the First Amendment in 1791 as a change in the law and claimed that Washington's attitudes did not change. Scholars, however, have pointed out that the Constitution itself established separation of church and state by Article VI: "no religious Test shall ever be required as a Qualification to any Office or public Trust under the United States." This placed all religions and no religion on an equal footing, and made it possible for churches and other religious institutions to thrive without favor or interference.

In summary, as the first President, Washington established at least seven important precedents on the place of religion in public life while maintaining the constitutional separation of church and state:

First: in his Inauguration he used a Bible, joined in prayers, and invoked God in his inaugural address;

Second: he issued Proclamations of Thanksgiving and Prayer, both in 1789, after the Constitution had been adopted and the federal government installed, and in 1795 when the "whiskey rebellion" had been suppressed;

Third: he supported military chaplains and chaplains for the Congress, paid for by public funds;

Fourth: he recognized the importance of religion and morality, as evidenced by the institution of the Northwest Ordinance and his own addresses, especially the Farewell Address;

Fifth: in his speeches and writings he made reference to God as "Providence," and used other religious language that was not Christian-specific and applied to all religious groups;

Sixth: he supported religious freedom or freedom of conscience, as expressed in letters to Quakers, Jews, Roman Catholics, and Baptists, all groups that occupied a minority status and had been subjected to persecution and discrimination;

Seventh: he showed restraint regarding the matter of financial aid to religion, one exception being his support of missionaries to help pacify Indian or Native American tribes.

6. *Papers of George Washington: Presidential Series*, 4:132

It would be foolish to speculate on how Washington would deal with Church-State issues today, especially in public schools, which did not exist in his lifetime. Suffice it to say that he sought a balance of "no establishment" and "free exercise," recognizing that neither was absolute.

Conclusion

George Washington was an imposing and popular figure in early American history, much loved and admired by his fellow citizens. Despite his limited education he held his own with the "best and brightest" leaders of the era, Benjamin Franklin, Thomas Jefferson, John Adams, and Alexander Hamilton. Besides being a great statesman, he was an innovative farmer and an early entrepreneur. His leadership in gaining independence from Great Britain, his presiding over the Constitutional Convention and supporting ratification, and his two terms as the first President, all rightly entitle him to be called "the father of his country." The people wanted to make him King, but he showed again and again by his farewells that he could never accept that title in a republic that renounced royal authority and the divine right of kings. His character and contributions have been celebrated in song and story. At his death he was almost deified.

In addition to the issue of slavery, religion and the separation of church and state have remained controversial issues in his life. Michael and Jana Novak, and Mary V. Thompson have pointed out that he was a lifelong Anglican/Episcopalian, was a man of prayer as well as charity, used biblical and religious language in his writings, and established important precedents in the appropriate relationship between religion and public life, while maintaining the constitutional separation of church and state. They have arrived at three conclusions. First, Washington used the word "Providence" to describe the benevolent care of a just and merciful God. The word appears in the Bible in the Apocrypha in reference to a God as eternal, all-wise, and divine. (Washington would add "inscrutable.") Second, Washington laid the foundation of many customs and practices that we take for granted today, such as using the Bible and prayers at his inauguration, and issuing the first Thanksgiving proclamation in 1789, urging citizens "to acknowledge the providence of Almighty God."

Finally, he emphasized the importance of religious freedom, writing to the Jewish synagogue in Newport, Rhode Island in 1790:

"For happily the Government of the United States, which gives to bigotry no sanction, to persecution no assistance, requires only that they who live under its protection should demean themselves as good citizens in giving it on all occasions their effectual support." [7]

At the same time he wrote to all the clergy in Newport a response to their greetings:

"I am inexpressibly happy that by the smiles of divine Providence, my weak but honest endeavors to serve my country have hitherto been crowned with so much success, and apparently given such satisfaction to those in whose cause they were exerted. The same benignant influence, together with the concurrent support of all real friends to their country will still be necessary to enable me to be in any degree useful to this numerous and free People over whom I am called to preside. Wherefore I return you, Gentlemen, my hearty thanks for your solemn invocation of Almighty God that every temporal and spiritual blessing may be dispensed to me, and that, under my administration, the families of these states may enjoy peace and prosperity, with all the blessings attendant on civil and religious liberty." [8]

The new nation was fortunate to have as its first President a leader who believed in the providential care of God, who promoted freedom of religion and conscience, who supported the separation of church and state, and established precedents on the role of religion in American public life that have remained with us to this day.

7. *Papers of George Washington: Presidential Series*, 6:285

8. Ibid, 6:279

CHAPTER 3

Lest We Forget

MEMORIAL DAY

IN THE WEEKEND SECTION of a local newspaper there was an article on Memorial Day which announced the unofficial beginning of the summer, when people should dust off their grill and dig out their Hawaiian shirts. It also mentioned the somber reason for the beginning of Memorial Day, to honor those who had given their lives in the service of their country.

Memorial Day is in danger of becoming a forgotten holiday. For many people, it is another long weekend, the first weekend to get away to the lakes, beaches, resorts, and summer cottages. For a smaller number, veterans' organizations and bands and town officials (and in my town, the volunteer fire department and ladies auxiliary), it is a day for a parade and the decoration of cemeteries where the dead of past wars are buried.

Years ago the editor of the magazine, *Christianity Today* asked: "How many people will take any of the reasons for commemoration into account when deciding how to spend Monday? The great temptation is to look at it simply as a day off from work, a part of a long weekend, the kick-off day for summer. For many, Memorial Day means opening up the summer home, or taking the first camping trip of the year, or launching the picnic season. In recent years Americans have gone to doing their own thing to such an extent that little is left of the old-fashioned community commemorations."[1]

Memorial Day has also become a generic day for remembering all those who have died. A pastor in one church issued a reminder every year in the Sunday bulletin early in May that on Memorial Day Sunday "we will

1. *Christianity Today*, (May 24, 1974) 34

once again set aside time during our worship service to remember those in our church family who are deceased. If you have a loved one whom you wish to have remembered, please contact the pastor." Many people responded to this invitation and on the Sunday immediately before Memorial Day a four-page insert with eighty-two names was printed in the bulletin, and during the service there was a time for remembering and a memorial prayer. This is only one example of a widespread practice. It is a fitting and proper thing to remember and memorialize those who have died; one of the finest characteristics of human beings is that we hold in our hearts and minds those who have preceded us in life and on whose shoulders we stand.

However, in a 2002 issue of the magazine of the Veterans of Foreign Wars one veteran wrote: "Memorial Day is supposed to be a day to remember and honor the nation's war dead. Lately, however, it has become a convenient day also to remember most everyone else."[2] The various religious communities have special days and ceremonies to remember the deceased. Christians, for example, observe All Saints Day, the first Sunday of November, as a day of remembrance.

The Origin and Purpose of Memorial Day

The roots of Memorial Day, or what was originally called Decoration Day, go back to the Civil War or the War Between the States. Women in the South were decorating graves before the war was over. Thousands of people gathered in May 1865 at a brand new cemetery in Charleston, South Carolina, for sermons, singing, and a picnic. It is reported that in 1867 women in the town of Columbus, Mississippi, said prayers and laid flowers on the graves of both Union and Confederate soldiers who were killed in the battle of Shiloh. The 1867 song, "Kneel where our loves are sleeping," was dedicated to the ladies of the South who are decorating the graves. In fact, many communities throughout the North and South claim to be the birthplace of Memorial Day. One such place is Boalsburg, Pennsylvania, because ceremonies were held at the local cemetery in October 1864, and July 4, 1865. However, the U.S. Congress voted in May 1966 to give the honor to Waterloo, New York, because of their well-publicized and continuous observance of the day through the initiative of druggist Henry C. Welles.

According to Drew Gilpin Faust, president of Harvard University, the origins of Memorial Day shouldn't be claimed by any one town, but

2. *VFW Magazine*, 89 (11) 6

should be shared by many communities as people in various parts of the country recognized the need to memorialize the dead soldiers and "restore the dignity of those lives," since they had died so far from home and in such a gruesome manner. In her book, *This Republic of Suffering: Death and the American Civil War*, she has examined the unimaginable death of so many soldiers in the context of the Victorian period emphasis on the "Good Death."

Carbondale, Illinois, had its first ceremony on April 29, 1866, and General John A. Logan was the principal speaker. This may have inspired him as Commander in Chief of the Grand Army of the Republic, to designate May 30, 1868, as a day "for the purpose of strewing with flowers or otherwise decorating the graves of comrades who died in defense of their country." It was called Decoration Day, and it was the hope of the General that it would be kept up from year to year and that graves would be decorated with the choicest flowers of springtime. The first Memorial Day exercises at Arlington National Cemetery were held that year, and the graves of both Union and Confederate soldiers were decorated. This tradition has continued ever since.

Since the Grand Army of the Republic was the veterans' organization of the Union Army, the designation of May 30 as Decoration Day was not accepted by southern states which had formed the Confederate States of America in 1861. According to the U.S. Department of Veterans Affairs, many of these states have selected different dates for honoring Confederate veterans. Arkansas and Texas observe January 19 (Texas as Confederate Heroes Day); Alabama, Florida, Georgia, Mississippi, and Texas observe the fourth or last Monday of April; North Carolina and South Carolina chose May 10; Virginia's is the last Monday of May; and Louisiana, Tennessee, and Kentucky set aside June 3. Shelby Foote, the Mississippi-born historian and chronicler of the Civil War, wrote that Memorial Day "hopscotched the calendar in the South," each state making its own choice. These days were observed by the United Confederate Veterans Association, which was founded in 1889 from various state organizations and other groups, as well as by descendants, such as the Sons of the Confederate Veterans and the United Daughters of the Confederacy.

The Grand Army of the Republic called it Memorial Day for the first time in 1882, but the term, "Decoration Day," was still used. After World War I the day was enlarged to include those who had died in all American wars, and in 1967 it was declared a federal holiday by the U.S. Congress. It was also changed from May 30 to the last Monday of May. There have been efforts to go back to the original date of May 30. For example, the Veterans of Foreign Wars declared in its 2002 Memorial Day address that changing the holiday to a three-day weekend undermines the meaning of the day and contributes to "the general public's nonchalant observance of Memorial Day." Legislation has been proposed in both houses of Congress to restore the original date and the bills have been referred to committees, but no action has been taken. A "National Moment of Remembrance" resolution was passed in 2000, asking that all Americans pause at 3 p.m. on Memorial Day "To voluntarily and informally observe in their own way a moment of remembrance and respect, pausing from whatever they are doing for a moment of silence or listening to Taps."

Observing Memorial Day

Everyone has memories of Memorial Day, a quintessential American day along with the Fourth of July and Thanksgiving. The day has been observed with picnics and parades, pageants and programs, family outings and reunions, amusement parks and ballgames, the Indy 500 or local racetracks. A typical small town will set aside the day with a parade that includes an honor guard, bands, political leaders, Boy and Girl Scouts, fire departments and their auxiliaries, local clubs and organizations, schools, religious and ethnic groups, historical societies and hereditary patriotic societies, local merchants, the local American Legion, VFW, or other veterans, and lots of proud citizens waving the American flag. The day may include a trip to the local cemetery for the laying of flowers, wreaths and flags, and the playing of "Taps," which is based on a French bugle signal. It also goes back to the Civil War and was first played at military funerals during the war, including the one for the Confederate General "Stonewall" Jackson. A ceremony on the town green concludes the day, with prayers, songs, the recital of "In Flanders Field" or the "Gettysburg Address," the honoring of Gold Star Mothers, wreath-laying at a Civil War monument, and a brief address.

My grandmother married a Civil War veteran, and she recalled how proudly he marched each Memorial Day with the Grand Army of the Republic in Great Barrington, Massachusetts. Each year our family brought flowers to the cemetery where he is buried, a tradition that continues to the present day. As a boy in seventh and eighth grade I took piano lessons and will never forget the tears that came to my grandmother's eyes when I played songs like "They're tenting tonight on the old campground," "Tramp, tramp, tramp," and "The battle cry of freedom." For several years a minister planned a Memorial Day Sunday featuring a dialogue sermon with a Dixieland jazz band, and the band played old favorites like "When the roll is called up yonder," "Just a closer walk with thee," and, of course, "When the saints go marching in." At the close of the service the band would lead the congregation outside to the Civil War monument on the Green.

The author Mary Ellen Chase remembered the Memorial Days of her youth in a small Maine village near Penobscot Bay. She described the procession from the town hall to the cemetery, led by the village band and followed by organizations and children carrying bouquets of flowers "to place upon the graves of our honored dead when once the procession with a final roll of drumbeats should halt in the cemetery and the signal should be given."[3]

One of the most ambitious studies of the symbols and rituals of Memorial Day was contained in volume five of the extensive Yankee City series done by W. Lloyd Warner and his colleagues. It was the result of an examination between 1930 and 1935 of the holiday observances in Newburyport, Massachusetts. Although the study was done of a northern community, its findings could be duplicated in cities and towns all over the country. Warner's purpose was to use anthropological and sociological methods to study the symbol systems and sacred traditions of Memorial Day, concluding that these forms ritually unite the living with the dead. The study examined the weeks of preparation by the different religious, ethnic and community groups and how they all came together in a unified ceremony. The rituals included a parade, wreaths, prayers, speeches, music, recitations, salutes, firing, and Taps. The theme was the sacrifice of life for the country. When the study was conducted in the early 1930s, there were still some veterans of the Civil War alive and they were treated like "spiritual beings." For many years the study was regarded as out of date because of its overemphasis on class and other distinctions, but it has received new interest because of a focus on civil religion, and Warner's study of Memorial Day was included in the 1974 book, *American Civil Religion*, edited by Russell Ritchey and Donald Jones.

What Warner and company have done in prose, Charles Ives has set to music. Although his career was in insurance, Ives was profoundly influenced by his father, who led the Danbury cornet band in Connecticut.

3. Chase. "Memorial Day 1900," *Ladies Home Journal*, LXXIV (May 1957), 145

One piece of music that Ives composed was a symphony called "Four New England Holidays," and the second movement was called "Decoration Day." The movement began early in the morning with the gathering of flowers. There was a distant bell ringing, a train whistle, and the chirping of birds. The village band played a kind of dirge on the way to the cemetery, and after the last grave was decorated a bugler played Taps and a hymn was sung. There was rousing martial music on the way back to the center of town. Ives's father was a Civil War bandmaster and veteran, and it is said that the Taps may well have been in his memory. In its entirety, the Ives symphony expressed a deep sense of patriotism and sought to arouse a feeling of nostalgia for past glory and an earlier, simpler life.

If Warner did it in prose and Ives in music, Norman Rockwell has put it all in a piece of art on the cover of *The Saturday Evening Post* for May 17, 1917. Shown in this dramatic drawing is a bearded Civil War veteran bedecked with medals and waving his hat. On his right is a woman dressed in white and on the left a young Boy Scout in full regalia and saluting. On the dress of the woman is the shadow of the American flag as it is carried down the street by the color guard in the parade. The threesome could well represent the three generations of my family, Civil War grandfather, daughter, and grandson.

A newer Memorial Day tradition not mentioned by Warner, Ives, or Rockwell is the red poppy. In 1915 John McCrae, a Canadian Colonel and surgeon, wrote a poem which expressed his sorrow over the "row on row" of graves of soldiers who were buried in the fields of Flanders, part of Belgium and northern France during World War I. He mentioned the bright red flowers growing among the crosses and urged his comrades on. It was intended as a call to arms against the enemy, not primarily a verse to be memorized by schoolchildren. The poem concluded with the words:

> "Take up our quarrel with the foe:
> To you from falling hands we throw
> The torch; be yours to hold it high.
> If ye break faith with us who die
> We shall not sleep, though poppies grow
> In Flanders fields."[4]

A woman in the state of Georgia, Moina Michael, was inspired by the poem and wrote her own poem about cherishing the "Poppy red," and she

4. *In Flanders Fields and Other Poems*, 3

thought of wearing red poppies on Memorial Day to honor those who died during the war. She was joined by a woman from France, Anna Guerin, who had come to the United States, and together they convinced the VFW to become the first group of veterans to sell the poppies for the benefit of war orphans. Now, veterans in medical facilities, hospitals, and nursing homes make the artificial flowers each year, keeping the tradition alive.

The American Civil War

The American Civil War has never been forgotten. Indeed, sometimes it seems that it never ended! No war in the history of this country has so occupied the attention or absorbed the energy of people like the Civil War. There is a never-ending debate as to whether the war could have been avoided, as well as over its meaning and purpose. For northerners, it was a war of southern rebellion; for southerners, it was a war of northern (or Yankee) aggression and invasion. The original purpose for the North was to preserve the Union; for the South, it was to preserve their culture and way of life. The underlying cause was the existence of slavery, and the impossibility of finding a compromise. The purpose, for the North at least, evolved into a war of liberation or emancipation of slaves, especially after January 1, 1863, when the Emancipation Proclamation went into effect.

According to James M. McPherson, in his Introduction to Bruce Catton's *The Civil War*, thousands of people gather every month in 250 Civil War Roundtables in places all over the country. About 40,000 re-enactors put on the blue or gray uniforms each year to stage encampments and mock battles. Millions visit the many Civil War battlefields and museums. Struggles continue over the flying of the Confederate flag and the designation by states of Confederate History Month. There are continuing fights to preserve the battlefields from housing developments, shopping malls, and amusement parks. A paper, *Civil War News*, is published each month in Vermont and is joined by countless other journals, magazines, newsletters, and blogs.

A documentary by Ken Burns on the Civil War was the most popular and well-received of his productions, with an estimated forty million viewers. Since *Gone with the Wind*, many movies, mini-series, and documentaries have been made on the Civil War era; a more recent one, *Glory*, about an African-American regiment from Massachusetts, achieved great acclaim. New books and articles fly from the presses each year; more has been published about the Civil War than any other event in American history. Courses are taught in schools and colleges; historians are in demand for lectures; and conferences are well attended. There are those people who can draw a diagram by memory of every detail of the three-day battle at Gettysburg, including Little Round Top, the Devil's Den, the Wheatfield, and Cemetery Ridge.

There have been over 50,000 books written about the Civil War, and the number increases every year. Foremost among the authors are four whose writings have received numerous prizes and awards and have hit the best-seller lists. Two were primarily journalists, Allan Nevins and Bruce Catton. A third, Shelby Foote, worked as both a journalist and a novelist. The fourth, James McPherson, devoted his life to the teaching of history. All four succeeded in developing not only the military aspects of the war, but the economic, social, and political issues as well. Two of them have lobbied against commercial developments in the areas of Civil War battlefields.

The Tragedy and Legacy of the Civil War

The Civil War was a tragedy. No effort to romanticize or glamorize the war can change the fact that it was the deadliest war in American history. Drew Gilpin Faust, pointing out how impossible it was to arrive at an accurate number of fatalities, wrote that estimates of the war dead have risen in recent years from 620,000 to 750,000. This number surpasses the grand total of fatalities of all other wars in the country's history. A majority of them died from sickness and disease. This does not count the number of civilians killed; one estimate used by McPherson is 50,000. In the twenty-first century the country mourned over 5,400 killed in Iraq and Afghanistan in the first decade. A "Field of Flags" traveled from town to town, with each flag representing a soldier who died. In the twentieth century it was reported that 2,000 were killed in one week in Vietnam. Yet at the Civil War battle of Cold Harbor, Virginia, 7,000 men were killed in one hour. A Confederate general named Evander Law is quoted as saying: "It was not war, but murder." There were 23,000 killed, wounded, or missing in one day in the battle of Antietam, Maryland. Accounts of the battles fought at Fredericksburg, Chancellorsville, and elsewhere tell of soldiers climbing over the bodies of dead soldiers, of rivers turned red by blood, of battlefields carpeted with the dead and dying.

At a 1994 conference on "Religion and the American Civil War" at Louisville Theological Seminary the question was raised as to why no one had studied the war from a "just war" perspective. Harry S. Stout, professor at Yale University, accepted the challenge and in 2006 wrote *Upon the Altar of the Nation: A Moral History of the Civil War*. According to Stout, just war theory developed at least 2,000 years ago to design ethical standards for war, but was codified by Thomas Aquinas in the thirteenth century. It involved principles for declaring war, only for defense, and for waging wars, principles of proportionality and discrimination. According to a strict interpretation of the theory, the Civil War was unjust, because of the destruction of life and property and the targeting of civilians. Stout showed that the approach of the Union Army was of "total war," and it was illustrated by the tactics of General Philip Sheridan in the Shenandoah Valley, by General William T. Sherman in Atlanta, Georgia, and South Carolina, and even by General "unconditional surrender" Ulysses S. Grant.

The strategy was a "scorched earth" one, in which food, livestock, homes and barns, railroads and factories, roads and bridges, and cities were destroyed, leaving no possibility for life or livelihood. For example, in regard to Sheridan's destruction of the Shenandoah Valley, Stout has quoted Grant's command: to turn "the Shenandoah Valley (into) a barren waste . . . so that crows flying over it for the balance of this season will have to carry their provender with them."[5] In another century these generals could have been indicted for war crimes. But the same could be said for those who ran the prisoner of war camps such as the infamous Andersonville. In spite of all this, both sides believed that their fallen soldiers were martyrs for the cause.

Two contemporaries witnessed the terrible tragedy of the Civil War and recorded it, one in photography and the other in print. Mathew Brady (1822–1896) was born in Warren County, New York, near Lake George, and early learned the art of photography from Samuel F. B Morse and others. He became the most famous photographer of his time and recorded for posterity the likeness of every U.S. President from John Quincy Adams to William McKinley, with the exception of William Henry Harrison, who died in office before Brady was active. His photographs of Lincoln are the most famous in existence. During the Civil War he set up studios in New York City and Washington, DC, and sent teams of photographers out into the battlefields with a kind of "traveling darkroom." As a result, the Civil

---

5. Stout, *Upon the Altar of the Nation*, 380

War became the first war in history to be recorded on film. Brady's exhibit at his New York City gallery in October 1862, "The Dead of Antietam," turned the stomachs of viewers with the graphic images of piles of corpses. For many people it brought close to home the horror and carnage of the war. After the war people lost interest in the photos, Brady was forced into bankruptcy, and it was not until 1912 that his photos were published as *The Photographic History of the Civil War.*

Walt Whitman (1819–1892) was born in Huntington, Long Island, New York, and worked as a journalist and writer (*Leaves of Grass),* teacher, government clerk, and as a volunteer nurse in the Civil War. He estimated that he visited and tried to help about 100,000 sick, wounded, or dying soldiers in hospitals in Washington, DC, and was profoundly moved by their pitiful conditions and amputated limbs. With voluminous notes collected in dozens of packets, he put down on paper his recollections and published them in two books. One was *Memoranda During the War* in 1875, and the other was *Specimen Days and Collect* in 1882, which included essays on trips, nature, and other writers. He recorded his encounters with about fifty soldiers, describing their suffering and agony. One of these soldiers in Campbell Hospital was my grandfather, Henry Decatur Boardman of the Twenty-Seventh regiment, Connecticut Volunteers, who was so sick and debilitated after the battle of Fredericksburg that he could not eat for days. In an entry called "A Connecticut Case" in the 1882 book, Whitman described how he found some home-made rice pudding for my grandfather, the only thing that he could eat.

The tragedy of the war was brought home in many personal ways. In my hometown Joseph L. Gomez has written a book, *Not in Vain: A Story of a Soldier,* which told about a young man who served in the Sixth Regiment, Connecticut Volunteers. He fell in love with a young teacher, and they were going to get married after the war. They wrote letters to each other sharing their hopes and dreams. He was badly wounded in the battle of Deep River, near the James River in Virginia, died in an army hospital in the Brooklyn area, and was buried on Long Island. His last letter to his girlfriend was found in his breast pocket after his death. He wrote:

> "My Dear Josie, I write this letter to you in the evening before a battle. I have a strange and uneasy feeling about tomorrow's fight . . . Please know that I will always love you, and though I have never held you in an embrace, I still feel that we are as close as any two people can be! . . . I ask that you do not grieve for me, but

that you go on and share your goodness with all about you as you always have. I am reminded of that Scottish poet you introduced me to, so long ago, in that little schoolhouse of ours in Prospect. He said, I believe, 'Of the words in speech or pen, The saddest are what might have been.' Farewell dear Josie, I have loved you long and well! Luzerne."[6]

This sad story was repeated thousands and thousands of times, as families in both North and South lost their loved ones—fathers, sons, brothers, sweethearts, friends and neighbors.

The tragedy of the Civil War was not only in lives lost or permanently maimed, property destroyed, cities and towns laid waste, but also in the fact that it did not ultimately succeed in opening up the voting franchise to a great portion of the American population. Despite amendments to abolish slavery and provide "due process," it would take another century before African-Americans were granted full citizenship rights.

Despite the tragedy, the legacy of the war was so profound that it would take (and has taken) volumes to explain. The Civil War has been called the "Second American Revolution." Because of the war, the United States became a single whole nation, rather than a federation of sovereign states. James McPherson was fond of pointing out that before the war one said "The United States *are*," but after the war, "The United States *is*." Before the war it was believed that states could secede from the Union. The New England states almost did at the Hartford Convention of 1812, or South Carolina in the nullification crisis of the 1830s. By 1861 eleven states did secede, but there has been no such action since. Not only did the United States become unified, but also developed a strong, centralized government. Again, McPherson has pointed out that six of the next seven amendments to the U.S. Constitution served to enlarge and strengthen the central government, expanding its powers. Before the war citizens were aware of a federal government through a postal service. After the war the lives of all Americans were impacted by an internal revenue service, military draft, regulation of commerce and industry, and a myriad other laws and bureaucracies.

Some of the legacy was political. Before the war the southern states controlled the U.S. Congress, the Supreme Court, and the Presidencies; after the war it was northern Republicans, and the period of Reconstruction did not bring about the kind of reunion and reconciliation that Lincoln

6. Gomez, *Not in Vain*, 143

had envisioned. The "total war" was continued with the near annihilation of Native Americans. Throughout the rest of the nineteenth century most of the Presidents were former Union Army Generals or a Brevet Major. The economic legacy was enormous. Industrial might and power mushroomed to meet the need for armaments, goods, and services; corporations blossomed; roads and railroads multiplied; great fortunes were made, leading to what has been called the "gilded age."

Where can one begin to describe the social impact? Because the Confederacy recognized God in their new Constitution, there was a concerted effort to pass a "Christian amendment" to the U.S. Constitution, but a compromise was arrived at, namely to adopt "In God we trust" as a motto and put it on the nation's coinage. The Social Gospel of the churches had its start with the work done by the Freedmen's Bureau and other agencies to help newly freed slaves. The American Red Cross had its beginnings with Clara Barton and her work as a nurse. A kind of religion of "The Lost Cause" permeated the South, with the belief that God was using defeat as an instrument of purging and cleansing. For veterans of the war there was the search for another cause to fight for, a kind of "moral equivalent of war."

God's Providential Working in History

Mark A. Noll, in his 2006 book, *The Civil War as a Theological Crisis*, has pointed out that during the war both sides claimed that God was on their side. Lincoln rephrased the question: "Are we on God's side?" He stated that the purposes of the Almighty are inscrutable, and that both sides bore responsibility for the conflict—the South because of its embrace of chattel slavery, the North because of its complicity.

Abraham Lincoln knew the heartbreak and tragedy of the Civil War as few others did. As President during those fateful years he faced the momentous decision of preserving the Union and committing the human and financial resources of the nation to that task. In one of his volumes on Lincoln, Carl Sandburg told how on the train to Gettysburg to deliver his immortal address, an elderly gentleman got on the train and told the President he had lost a son at Little Round Top at Gettysburg. The President answered that he feared a visit to that spot would open fresh wounds, and yet if the end of sacrifice had been reached "we could give thanks even amidst our tears." Then Lincoln is quoted as unburdening his soul to this man: "When I think of the sacrifices of life yet to be offered, and the hearts and homes yet to be made desolate before this dreadful war is over, my heart is like lead within me, and I feel at times like hiding in deep darkness."[7]

It is in this context that we can appreciate the lines from the Gettysburg Address: "But, in a larger sense, we cannot dedicate, we cannot consecrate, we cannot hallow, this ground. The brave men, living and dead, who struggled here, have consecrated it, far above our power to add or to detract. The world will very little note nor long remember what we say here, but it can never forget what they did here." The world has both noted and remembered what was said that day at Gettysburg, and it has never forgotten what was done there.

Lincoln had a profound understanding of the judgment of God. His second Inaugural Address is not only one of the masterpieces of the English language, but also a great religious statement, reflecting the words of the Hebrew prophets:

> "Fondly do we hope—fervently do we pray—that this mighty scourge of war may speedily pass away. Yet, if God wills that it continue, until all the wealth piled by the bondman's two hundred and fifty years of unrequited toil shall be sunk, and until every drop of blood drawn with the lash shall be paid by another drawn with the sword, as was said three thousand years ago, so still it must be said: 'the judgments of the Lord are true and righteous altogether.'
>
> "With malice toward none; with charity for all; with firmness in the right as God gives us to see the right, let us strive on to finish the work we are in; to bind up the nation's wounds; to care for him who shall have borne the battle, and for his widow, and his orphan—to do all which may achieve and cherish a just, and a lasting peace, among ourselves, and with all nations."[8]

Lest we forget the original meaning and purpose of Memorial Day. Lest we forget the tragedy and legacy of the Civil War. Lest we forget the God who rules history, who judges people and nations by a righteous will declared through prophets and apostles. Lincoln referred at Gettysburg to this nation *under* God. The danger is that powerful nations will forget that they are under the judgment of God, that if they place all their faith in armies and navies and air power, in missiles and guns and bombs, they may go the way of other nations.

7. Sandburg, *Abraham Lincoln: The War Years*, 405

8. Lincoln, *Speeches and Writings*, 2:687

Julia Ward Howe wrote movingly of the judgment of God in her poem, which we know as the "Battle Hymn of the Republic." Especially in the second verse:

> "He has sounded forth the trumpet that shall never call retreat;
> he is sifting out all human hearts before his judgment seat;
> O be swift, my soul, to answer him; be jubilant, my feet!
> Our God is marching on.
> Glory, glory, hallelujah! Glory, glory, hallelujah! Glory, glory hallelujah!
> His truth is marching on."[9]

As we enjoy our picnics and parades, our beaches and barbecues, let us remember the original meaning and purpose of Memorial Day, the tragedy and legacy of the Civil War, the sacrifices of those who fought and died in all the wars of our country. Lest we forget that God judges all nations; in the words of that old hymn, "tho' the wrong seems oft so strong, God is the ruler yet," that it is God who rules history, that despite all of mankind's warring madness, God's plan and purpose will be worked out, ushering in a kingdom of love and righteousness, of peace and justice.

9. Howe, "Battle Hymn of the Republic" (1861)

CHAPTER 4

What So Proudly We Hailed

FLAG DAY, JUNE 14

THE UNITED STATES IS a country that wraps itself in a flag, what one historian has called a "uniquely flag-centered patriotism." From an ensign or banner carried on ships, the American flag has evolved into the supreme and sacred symbol of the nation. After the tragedy of September 11, 2001, cars and trucks, homes and barns, bridges and towers, buildings and shopping malls were bedecked with the "stars and stripes," signifying not only a country in mourning but a country with pride, resolve and determination. "Old Glory" has been carried by Americans on boundless seas, rugged hills, volcanic islands, steamy jungles, endless deserts, remote villages, and war-torn cities. It flew through the night at Fort McHenry, was planted on the North Pole by Robert Peary in 1909, on Mt. Everest by James Whittaker in 1963, and on the moon by Neil Armstrong in 1969, was raised by the Marines on Mount Suribachi at Iwo Jima, and survived the bombing of the World Trade Center. In July 2010 it was reported that two spaceships, Voyager I and II, both launched in 1977, were headed beyond our solar system into the far reaches of space with American flags on board.

The American flag is unique among the nations of the world: it has a birthday, an anthem, a march, songs, a pledge, a salute, and an elaborate protocol regarding its use and careful disposal when tattered and torn. Around the "Star-Spangled Banner" has clustered a host of stories and legends which encompass the entire history of the country. The names of larger-than-life figures will be forever linked with the flag: Betsy Ross, Francis Scott Key, John Philip Sousa, and George M. Cohan. There have also been a number of organizations and lesser known individuals who have worked and lobbied for school flags, a pledge, laws, a code, and a national Flag Day. It has been the subject for countless artists and composers and has inspired poets, preachers, and presidents. The flag is raised over American Olympic winners, and winning athletes literally wrap themselves in the flag for a victory lap around the stadium.

Flag Day is not a federal holiday nor a day off from work or school, yet it possesses a mystique and character all its own. It was on June 14, 1777, that the Continental Congress meeting in Philadelphia passed a resolution offered by John Adams that "the flag of the United States be thirteen stripes, alternating red and white, that the Union be thirteen white stars in a blue field representing a new constellation." The U.S. Congress passed another resolution in 1794, after Vermont and Kentucky had joined the Union, that the flag should have fifteen stars and fifteen stripes, and thus it stayed until 1818 when a third resolution was passed keeping the stripes at thirteen in a horizontal fashion but adding a star for each new state, with the provision: "That on the admission of every state into the Union, one star be added to the union of the flag, and that such addition shall take effect on the fourth of July next succeeding such admission."

A day to celebrate the flag was not suggested until 1861 in Hartford, Connecticut, but a teacher in Wisconsin and an educator/textbook author in Pennsylvania started a movement in the 1880s and 1890s to establish a national Flag Day. Other people and groups joined in. President Woodrow Wilson officially proclaimed Flag Day in 1916 and President Calvin Coolidge in 1927, but it wasn't until 1949 that a National Flag Day was established by an act of Congress.

The Evolution of the American Flag

The American flag hasn't stood still. In the history of this country there have been twenty-seven different designs of the flag, including the most recent change in 1960 after Alaska was added to the Union. There have been many books on the history and design of the flag. Since World War II several have stood out. One of the most detailed and carefully researched was the book published by the Smithsonian Institution in 1981 entitled *So Proudly We Hail: The History of the United States Flag*, written by two career naval officers, Rear Admiral William Rae Furlong and Commodore Byron McCandless.

One of the most beautiful coffee table-style books was published by the National Geographic Society in 1993 and was written by Margaret Sedeen, staff writer and editor. The book is organized in four major sections: the birth of the flag, the flag in war and diplomacy, in exploration, and in daily life. Also included is a final section on flag etiquette. Complementing the text are numerous glossy photographs, which bring the events to life. In spite of the changes in the flag over the years, the author felt that the response of people to the flag has been constant, that it has been looked upon with reverence, pride, and joy. This is in spite of the fact that the flag has been used for political campaigns, advertising, and demonstrations.

One of the most distinctive books about the flag was the 1973 volume, *The Stars and the Stripes: The American Flag as Art and History from the Birth of the Republic to the Present*, by Boleslaw and Marie-Louise D'Otrange Mastai. The authors have dispensed with the usual chronological order so that they could present the flag as folk art, often home-made and home-designed, as an expression of the creative spirit of the American people. Before the arrangement of the stars and stripes was codified in the twentieth century, people found artistic and inventive ways to present the stars in the blue canton and display the stripes.

Another contribution was the 1961 book, *The History of the United States Flag: From the Revolution to the Present, Including a Guide to Its Use and Display*, by historian Milo M. Quaife, joined by two members of the National Park Service, Melvin J. Weig and Roy E. Appleman.

In 1970 was published *The Flag Book of the United States: The Story of the Stars and Stripes and the Flags of the Fifty States*. The author was Whitney Smith, professor at Boston University and director of the Flag Research Center in Lexington, Massachusetts. What is unique about this book is the presentation of the development of the state flags, along with those of territories, cities, and Indian nations.

The most helpful book in understanding the changes over time in the meaning and significance of the flag was *The American Flag, 1777–1924: Cultural Shifts from Creation to Codification* by Scot M. Guenter, professor at San Jose State University. Guenter's work, published in 1990, showed that contributions of individuals, organizations and institutions had affected the changing use of the flag and feelings and sentiments toward it. Guenter found the concept of "American civil religion" to be useful, with the flag as a sacred symbol. The result was an historical overview of the cultural shifts in the presentation, reproduction and use of the flag, beginning with the first ones for a new nation up through the second flag conference of 1924, when the flag code was finalized.

All of these studies have come to important conclusions about the history of the flag, including the following:

The first flag of the continental army of the united colonies in 1775 under George Washington was the "Grand Union," consisting of thirteen stripes and the British Union Jack as the canton.

Betsy Ross did not design the first American flag, but it was Francis Hopkinson, a delegate from New Jersey to the Continental Congress, who submitted an invoice in 1780 for his work on the national flag, as well as the seal and other items. It was recognized that he did not act alone, but was one of the main consultants on the project.

The flag of the new United States took many forms during the Revolutionary War, and the stars and stripes did not assume a more recognizable form until the end of the war. It was more commonly displayed on ships and on military installations, and was not carried into battle by the U.S. Army until the Mexican War.

Artists like Jonathan Trumbull, who painted battle scenes, Archibald Willard, with his *The Spirit of '76,* and those who painted Betsy Ross with the stars in a circle were historically inaccurate in their depiction of the flag and yet they have influenced generations of Americans. They tended to paint the flag in the Revolutionary War period in a way that belonged to later periods of American history.

The flag that flew over Fort McHenry in Baltimore harbor in the War of 1812 was the flag authorized by the Congress in 1794 with fifteen stars and stripes. It was made by Mary Pickersgill, whose mother was Rebecca Young, a contemporary of Betsy Ross. It was at this time that Francis Scott Key wrote the poem that was set to music and became the national anthem.

During the Civil War, President Lincoln would not allow any of the stars to be removed from the flag because he never recognized that the Confederate states were out of the Union. The flag became something to die for.

Throughout the nineteenth and into the twentieth century the flag took on many shapes, sizes, and designs, representative of a great deal of artistic license and creative expression.

As a result of the nation's Centennial in 1876 and the work of veterans' organizations and hereditary patriotic societies there emerged in the late nineteenth century a "cult of the flag," with the symbol itself the object of veneration to be kept by law from any desecration.

Also, in the last decades of the nineteenth century there emerged movements to add flags to every school and classroom, introduce and promote a Pledge of Allegiance to the flag, and create a national Flag Day.

It was at the flag conferences of 1923 and 1924 that a standard design for the flag and an elaborate code for its use were developed, along with a revision of the Pledge. The words "under God" were not added to the Pledge until 1954.

The flag has been the subject of a number of Supreme Court decisions. In 1940 the court decided that school children could be required to recite the Pledge of Allegiance in their classrooms, but reversed itself three years later and ruled that a compulsory flag salute was contrary to the First Amendment and was unconstitutional. In 1989 and 1990 the court ruled that burning the flag in a demonstration was protected by the First Amendment right of free speech and was therefore constitutional.

Rather than a "constant" the meaning and significance of the American flag have changed in time, depending upon historical circumstances and cultural influence.

The Five Stages in the Meaning and Significance of the Flag

There have been at least five stages in the meaning and significance of the flag: In each stage there were myths, legends, and individuals that became an integral part of the telling of our country's history. Feelings and sentiments in each stage were carried over into successive stages.

1) The emblem of a new nation

It has been said that Americans have an endless fascination with the beginnings of things, in pinpointing the date and circumstances for our "accomplishments and institutions." This is why we are so enamored of the tale of a seamstress named Betsy Ross in revolutionary Philadelphia, who was reputed to have met with George Washington and others early in 1776 and designed the nation's first flag. Despite the fact that there is no historical documentation for the meeting, the story has lingered in our collective memory and in our history books, in part because of its charm and the fact that an otherwise unknown woman had become one of our "founding mothers."

The Betsy Ross legend became public in 1870, when one of her grandsons, William J. Canby, presented a paper to the Historical Society of Pennsylvania regarding the making of the first American flag, but he had first heard the story in 1857 from an elderly aunt before she moved to Iowa. The story was that in early June 1776 General Washington, Robert Morris and George Ross, a committee from the Continental Congress, had visited Betsy Ross at her shop in Philadelphia. They wanted her to design a flag for the new nation, and she showed them how a five-pointed star would be easier to make than a six-pointed star. Inaccuracies in the story are readily apparent. There was no committee of the Continental Congress appointed to design a new flag, there was not a new independent nation until July 2, 1776 (the Declaration was adopted on July 4), and it was not until June 14, 1777, that a resolution was passed to create a new flag. In other words, the American flag did not spring fully starred and striped from the fertile mind and nimble hands of Betsy Ross!

However, the legend was born and took on a life of its own. Charles A. Weisgerber, who knew the story told in 1870, painted the familiar "Birth of Our Nation's Flag," showing Betsy presenting the completed flag with the stars in a circle to the committee. This painting was exhibited at the great Columbian Exposition in Chicago in 1893, it became popular instantly, and many copies were distributed throughout the country. Weisgerber and others were involved in the creation of the Betsy Ross Memorial Association and the American Flag House, and the group was successful in the effort to save the Betsy Ross House on Arch Street in Philadelphia from demolition. It is visited by hundreds of thousands of tourists every year. Betsy Ross had become an integral part of the story of the beginnings of our country.

The real story is more interesting and complex. Marla R. Miller, professor at the University of Massachusetts in Amherst, has written what she called the "first scholarly biography" of Betsy Ross (1752–1836), *Betsy Ross and the Making of America*. Even though Betsy did not leave much of a paper trail, Miller has researched available family, church, public, newspaper and other records to come up with an account of a talented artisan who indeed made flags, hundreds of them, for the Pennsylvania Navy in 1777 and for the U.S. government to go on garrisons and trading posts throughout the country. According to Miller, she was representative of the hundreds and thousands of craftsmen and women who made America. Born Elizabeth

Griscom in Philadelphia, she was a "hand-shake" away from the "Founding Fathers," and was a part of the influential Society of Friends until she married her first husband, John Ross, an Anglican. Her first two husbands died in the Revolutionary War, Ross in a munitions explosion and Joseph Ashburn in a British prison. Her third marriage to John Claypoole lasted the longest and they lived to see their children grow up and become a part of her flourishing upholstery business. Miller wrote: "She is important to our understanding of American history not because she made any one flag, however iconic that moment may have become, but because she was a young craftswoman who embraced the resistance movement with vigor, celebrated its triumphs and suffered its consequences."[1]

2) Symbol of the survival of freedom and liberty

In the first half of the nineteenth century the flag moved from ships and garrisons into more public display as a symbol of freedom and liberty to be used in campaigns and demonstrations and extended to newly acquired land in the West. Playing an important part in this stage was the growing popularity of "The Star Spangled Banner," written in 1814 by Francis Scott Key (1779–1843). In the War of 1812 Great Britain, from which American independence had been won nearly 30 years earlier, invaded the United States, burned the Capitol and the Executive Mansion, and attacked Baltimore. As a lawyer, Key was attempting to free Dr. William Beanes, who had been captured by the British. Along with another American, Col. John Skinner, Key was detained on a British ship in Baltimore harbor during the bombardment of Fort McHenry on September 13–14, 1814. In the morning Key saw that the American flag was still flying over the fort, and on his way back to Baltimore he wrote the poem "The Defense of Fort McHenry." It was published in the newspaper on September 20 and set to the music of "To Anacreon in Heaven," a British drinking song. It became widely popular, was adopted by the Army and Navy, was declared a national anthem by Woodrow Wilson in 1916, but it wasn't made official until an act of Congress in 1931.

Francis Scott Key was born in Carroll County, Maryland, studied at St. John's College in Annapolis, and became a lawyer, arguing cases before the U.S. Supreme Court and serving as district attorney in Washington, DC. He had moved from Frederick to Georgetown, married Mary T. Lloyd, and

1. Miller, *Betsy Ross and the Making of America*, 361

they had eleven children. Key was an author, a poet, and a deeply religious person, serving as a vestryman and lay reader in the Episcopal Church. He served as vice president of the American Bible Society from 1817 until his death, and was an agent of the American Sunday School Union. Most people know by heart the first stanza of the national anthem, but it is the fourth verse which inspired a motto of the country, "In God we trust." The fourth stanza reads:

> "O, thus be it ever when freemen shall stand,
> Between their loved home and the war's desolation!
> Blest with victory and peace, may the heav'n-rescued land
> Praise the Power that hath made and preserved us a nation!
> Then conquer we must, when our cause, it is just,
> And this be our motto: 'In God is our trust.'
> And the star-spangled banner in triumph shall wave
> O'er the land of the free and the home of the Brave!"[2]

3) The sacred symbol of national unity

When the country was torn apart in the tragic Civil War, 1861–1865, the flag became a symbol of national unity and what has been called the "totem of American civil religion." It was an object to rally around, to guard tenaciously, to wave defiantly, and to risk one's life and die for. Among the many stories that emerged from the war, several will illustrate the emotive power of the flag. The war began when Confederate forces fired on Fort Sumter in Charleston harbor, South Carolina. The fort surrendered on April 14 and the flag was taken down, only to be displayed in New York City and elsewhere as a motivational tool to raise money, troops and enthusiasm for the war. Although not specifically composed at that time, George F. Root wrote in 1862 one of the most stirring songs of the war, "Battle Cry of Freedom," with the closing words: "While we rally 'round the flag, boys, rally once again, Shouting the battle cry of freedom." So popular was the song that it was sung by both sides of the conflict, with different words, of course.

One of the great stories that came out of the war concerned a retired sea captain, William Driver, who had flown the American flag for forty years at sea and had first called it "Old Glory." He had moved to Nashville,

---

2. Key, "Star Spangled Banner," (1814)

Tennessee, but when the state seceded from the Union, as a Union sympathizer, he hid the flag inside bed coverings. When Union troops took over Nashville early in 1862, Capt. Driver took the flag out of hiding and with an officer raised "Old Glory" over the State Capitol. Another story was told in the 1863 poem by John Greenleaf Whittier about an elderly woman in Frederick, Maryland, named Barbara Frietchie. General Thomas "Stonewall" Jackson and his army briefly occupied the town in 1862 and, according to the poem, shot down the American flag at her home. She rescued it and waved it defiantly, saying (according to the poem) "Shoot if you must this old gray head, But spare your country's flag, she said." The General reacted with "A shade of sadness, a blush of shame," and responded: "Who touches a hair of yon gray head, Dies like a dog! March on, he said."[3] Even though it was later reported that Jackson's troops never went by her house, and the woman who did wave the flag was named Mary Quantrell, the story of Barbara Frietchie's bravery and loyalty to the flag has inspired generations of Americans.

Many stories have been told about bravery and sacrifice on the battlefields of the war. My grandfather, Henry Decatur Boardman, a corporal with the Twenty-Seventh Regiment, Connecticut Volunteers, wrote a letter on December 17, 1862, to his sister after the bloody battle at Fredericksburg, Virginia. He wrote of the heroic efforts to save the flag, of soldiers risking their lives and dying for it. My grandfather wrote: "The color bearer had stuck the staff of the colors into the ground. They were about three rods from me. A shell came down in the midst of them and exploded, killing every one of them, but the colors still continued to wave over the dead, eight killed by a single shell."[4] (I had always wondered why his daughter, my mother, referred to the American flag as "the country's colors.")

4) Symbol of American Nationalism

At the end of the nineteenth century and the beginning of the twentieth there arose another cluster of meanings around the flag, as a symbol of American nationalism in the world. Having united itself after the Civil War, the country embarked on a campaign to flex its muscles and exert itself around the globe. This stage is identified especially with two U.S. Presidents, William McKinley and Theodore Roosevelt. One led the nation in

3. *A Library of Poetry and Song*, 448
4. Boardman, unpublished letter (Dec. 17, 1862)

the Spanish-American War, after which the U.S. acquired the Philippines, Guam, Cuba, and Puerto Rico, the trappings of empire. The second presided over the acquisition of the area in Panama to build a canal, a battle to put down an insurrection in the Philippines, and the sending of a "Great White Fleet" under the flag around the world in 1906–1907 to demonstrate American power and might, especially to impress the Japanese. This period in American history is marked by such expressions as "gunboat diplomacy," "send in the Marines," and "show the flag." The U.S. withdrew its troops from Cuba in 1902, but held onto Guantanamo Bay as a naval base. Puerto Rico has continued as a territory or "commonwealth" to this day, and Guam as a naval base, but the Philippines gained its independence after World War II. It can be argued that this stage has continued until the present time and is in conflict with the fifth stage.

5) Symbol of American Ideals and Values

In his April 2, 1917, address to Congress as the U.S. entered World War I against Germany, Woodrow Wilson said that the world must be made safe for democracy and peace founded on principles of political liberty. According to Wilson, the country desired no conquest or dominion. In effect, the President re-stated what had always been true of the country since its founding, a commitment to freedom and liberty for itself and for all peoples. The country's entry into the First and Second World Wars, and its alliance with other nations to stop invasions and totalitarian regimes were reflections of its highest ideals and values, while interference in other countries' civil wars was ill-advised and costly. In his first proclamation of Flag Day in 1981, Ronald Reagan said that "the American flag has embodied the continuity of our original ideals and principles." He quoted from the outstanding nineteenth century clergyman, Henry Ward Beecher, in conveying the full meaning of the flag: "A thoughtful mind, when it sees a nation's flag, sees not the flag only, but the nation itself, and whatever may be its symbols, its insignia, he reads chiefly in the flag the government, the principles, the truths, the history which belongs to the nation that sets it forth." [5]

In his 1996 proclamation of Flag Day President Bill Clinton referred to the nation's flag with the words, "There is no better symbol of our country's values and traditions." President George W. Bush began his 2005

5. Reagan, *Proclamation* 4846 (January 1, 1981)

proclamation with the following: "For more than two centuries, the flag of United States has been a symbol of hope and pride. The flag has inspired our citizens during times of conflict and comforted us during moments of sorrow and loss." [6]

"The Cult of the Flag"

Toward the end of the nineteenth century and in the beginning of the twentieth century there were six movements which created what has been called "the cult of the flag." The first was the campaign to add flags to every school in the country, and it was spearheaded by the largest veterans' organization, the Grand Army of the Republic, members of which had risked their lives for the flag in the Civil War. They were determined to teach respect and reverence for the flag to the nation's schoolchildren, especially at a time of an increasing immigrant population. The movement began modestly enough when the New York division of the G.A.R. proposed a law mandating flags for all schools. Public presentations started in 1888 and 1889. According to historian Guenter, the post commander said: "Let this dear old Flag be more sacred in your eyes, more entitled to your homage, more dear to your hearts . . . "[7] Flag presentations in other cities led to a decision at the national encampment of the G.A.R. in 1889 to make it a national policy and practice. The G.A.R. also worked to introduce flags into houses of worship. One Civil War veteran and Methodist pastor, George M. Gue in Rockland, Illinois, edited *Our Country's Flag,* a large collection of pictures, poems and quotations. One poem, "The Flag O'er Our School-House is Floating," showed the flag over the school as a symbol of the sacrifices made by soldiers in the Civil War.

A second movement added The Pledge of Allegiance to the schoolhouse flag ritual. The largest magazine in circulation in the country, *The Youth's Companion,* had supported the school flag program, and had sold many flags as a premium. The editors conceived of a nation-wide salute to the flag by schoolchildren on the 400th anniversary of the first Columbus landfall in 1892, in connection with the Columbian Exposition in Chicago. A young Baptist minister, Francis J. Bellamy, editor of *The Youth's Companion,* organized the program. He enlisted the support of the school superintendents and the National Education Association, became chairman of

6. Bush, *Proclamation of Flag Day,* (June 13, 2005)

7. Guenter, *The American Flag 1777–1924,* 105

the planning committee, received endorsements from two U.S. Presidents, Benjamin Harrison and Grover Cleveland, and a future one, Theodore Roosevelt. He pulled out all the stops in an ambitious public relations campaign, with press releases, circulars, editorials and articles, and wrote the Pledge of Allegiance himself.

The National Public School Celebration for Columbus Day had eight parts: President's Proclamation; raising of flag by veterans; salute to the flag; prayer; song (often "America"); address; ode or poem; and additional addresses and national songs. It was reported that 120,000 public schools participated in the program. Bellamy wrote the Pledge to go with the salute to the flag, which consisted of extending the right arm up to the flag with the palm upward. (This salute was changed in the early 1940s to a hand over the heart because it was too much like the Nazi salute.) The original pledge read: "I pledge allegiance to my Flag and the Republic for which it stands; one nation, indivisible, with liberty and justice for all." The term, allegiance, was borrowed from the Oath of Allegiance from the Civil War and Reconstruction period. In writing the Pledge, Bellamy said he was inspired by the Declaration of Independence, the Constitution, and the use of the word, "indivisible," by Lincoln and Daniel Webster.

A third movement, to prevent desecration of the flag, was led by the new patriotic hereditary societies, the Sons of the American Revolution (1889), the Colonial Dames of America (1890), the Daughters of the American Revolution (1890), and the Society of Mayflower Descendants (1894). The problem was the use or defacing of the flag in political campaigning and commercial advertising. To deal with the situation, the different societies formed flag committees, and this resulted in the American Flag Association, which sought to get federal legislation passed. When such efforts failed, the groups turned to the states; the first state to pass a law restricting the use of the flag was South Dakota in 1897, and other states followed. In 1907 the U.S. Supreme Court declared such laws to be constitutional.

A fourth movement, though not such an organized one, was the proliferation of popular music with patriotic themes. On the vaudeville circuit it was discovered that a closing act with a patriotic tableaux and song, with the American flag unfurled, could bring any show to a rousing climax. George M. Cohan, a veteran of vaudeville, took this enthusiasm to Broadway with his musicals, *Little Johnny Jones* in 1904, and *George Washington, Jr.* in 1906. The first hit featured the song "I'm a Yankee Doodle Dandy," and the second had "You're a Grand Old Flag." In 1896 John Philip Sousa, who had been the leader of the U.S. Marine Corps Band, composed "The Stars and Stripes Forever," which became a perennial favorite and finale at concerts. Sousa wrote the lyrics to his own march, and in the chorus had the following words:

> "Hurrah for the flag of the free!
> May it wave as our standard forever,
> The gem of the land and the sea,
> The banner of the right.
> Let despots remember the day
> When our fathers with mighty endeavor
> Proclaimed as they marched to the fray
> That by their might and by their right
> It waves forever."[8]

In the 1987 Broadway musical, *Teddy and Alice*, new lyrics were written to Sousa's march, and it was called "Wave The Flag." Irving Berlin had continued this musical patriotism earlier in the twentieth century with songs such as "God Bless America."

A fifth movement was to codify flag usage. On the invitation of the American Legion, two national flag conferences were held in Washington, DC, in 1923 and 1924, attended by representatives of many civilian and military organizations. A Flag Code was adopted for the proper use and display of the flag, and this was widely distributed throughout the country. Also, the wording of the Pledge of Allegiance was changed from "my flag" to "the flag of the United States of America."

The sixth and final movement was the creation of National Flag Day. Despite its beloved nature and many layers of meaning, it took almost ninety years for the flag to receive an official day. The earliest attempt at a Flag Day was in Hartford, Connecticut, in 1861 at the beginning of the Civil War. The centennial of the Flag Resolution of 1777 was celebrated in 1877. However, it was Bernard Cigrand, a grade school teacher in Waubeka, Wisconsin, who organized a program to observe Flag Day at the Stony Hill School in 1885. After he moved to Chicago to become a dentist, he wrote an article about the fourteenth of June, and it led to other articles and speeches. In 1894 there was a huge celebration in Chicago, and Cigrand became president of the American Flag Day Association. The one who organized the association was William T. Kerr, a native of Collier Township,

8. Sousa, "Stars and Stripes Forever," (1897)

Pennsylvania, who later moved to Yeadon, a suburb of Philadelphia. Kerr served as chairman of the association for fifty years and was invited to be present in 1949 when Harry S. Truman signed the act of Congress which made the day official. Both Cigrand and Kerr are recognized as the founders of Flag Day, and they are memorialized both in their hometowns and in their adopted towns.

There were others who contributed to the development of Flag Day. One was George Balch, a teacher in New York City, who organized a ceremony in 1889. Another was the Betsy Ross Memorial Association, which organized a Flag Day at the Betsy Ross House in Philadelphia. Elizabeth Duane Gillespie, president of the Colonial Dames of Pennsylvania, attempted to get the flag displayed on all public buildings in 1893. In 1907 the Benevolent and Protective Order of Elks designated June 14 as Flag Day and lobbied to get national recognition. In response, Woodrow Wilson proclaimed a Flag Day in 1916, but it was not until 1949 that the U.S. Congress passed legislation establishing the day and calling on the President to offer an annual Proclamation. Since 1966 these Proclamations have designated the entire week as National Flag Week.

One Nation Under God

By vote of the U.S. Congress, The words "under God," were added to the Pledge of Allegiance in 1954. When Dwight Eisenhower signed the act, he said that the country was reaffirming the "transcendence of religious faith in America's heritage and future," which he called its "spiritual weapons." From a theological point of view, this was a good addition, since it recognized that the country exists under the Providence and judgment of God. There were those who were unhappy with the change because it seemed to interrupt the rhythm and flow of the original Pledge. There were those who have suggested that the words were added because we were engaged in a cold war with what was perceived as godless Communism. There were also those who felt that this was a violation of the wall of separation between church and state, as guaranteed by the First Amendment. In California a father of a public school pupil brought suit against the addition, and in 2002 the Ninth U.S. Circuit Court of Appeals ruled that reciting the pledge was unconstitutional because "under God" had been added. Eight years later, in 2010, the Court reversed itself and a majority declared that the phrase was constitutional, since "The Pledge of Allegiance serves to unite our vast nation through the proud recitation of some of the ideals upon which our Republic was founded."[9]

The words "under God" in a pledge to the nation's flag do not establish or promote religion. The word "God" by itself does not determine a religion; there are many ideas and concepts of what God means. Instead, the words recognize the historic reference point of God throughout American history, whether the *Mayflower Compact* of the Pilgrims, the "New Israel" or "Promised Land" of the Puritans, the "Providence" of George Washington, the "Creator" and "Judge" in the Declaration of Independence, the "In God is our trust" of Francis Scott Key, or "this nation under God" of Lincoln's Gettysburg Address. To leave out any reference to God in relation to the flag and the Republic for which it stands is to ignore the facts of history and be blind to the history and heritage of this great country. It is to forget the sublime virtues and transcendent values for which soldiers of the Civil War and all other wars have fought, and to present some sanitized, politically correct version of our country's history.

At the same time, it would be foolish and arrogant to see the flag as the primary thing that we give allegiance or loyalty to. The flag is a symbol of our country; it reflects whatever meanings we ascribe to it: national beginnings and survival, unity, nationalism, ideals and values. What is distinctive about our flag is that it waves over a land of the free and the brave, over a land with liberty and justice for all, and these values were not bestowed by the country and its government, but by a God who rules in human history, and to whom all peoples and nations are accountable.

9. *Newdow v. Rio Linda Union School District*, Ninth U. S. Circuit Court (March 12, 2010)

CHAPTER 5

We Hold These Truths

INDEPENDENCE DAY—FOURTH OF JULY

In 1961 the Rev. David Redding of Glendale, Ohio, wrote a guest editorial, "The Faith of Our Fathers," in the weekly *LIFE* magazine, beginning this way: "The Fourth of July doesn't go to church . . . At its wildest, it acts like late Saturday night and in its solemn moments like a well-behaved civics class . . . Our picture of the Patriots and the 'Spirit of '76' was taken as they paraded noisily down the street. The racket they made has built up until it drowns out hymns and prayers to the author of liberty."[1] The author of this editorial is right. There is something incongruous about the quiet dignity of a religious or prayer service and the explosive bursts of fireworks, something incompatible about worship and the Fourth of July. Independence Day is not a religious holiday or a special day in any religious calendar.

John Adams wrote a letter to his wife, Abigail, on July 3, 1776, in which he said:

> "The second day of July, 1776, will be the most memorable epoch in the history of America. I am apt to believe that it will be celebrated by succeeding generations as the great anniversary festival. It ought to be commemorated as the day of deliverance, by solemn acts of devotion to God Almighty. It ought to be solemnized with pomp and parade, with shows, games, sports, guns, bells, bonfires and illuminations, from one end of this continent to the other, from this time forward forevermore."[2]

1. Redding, *LIFE* (June 30, 1961) 52
2. Shuffelton, ed, *The Letters of John and Abigail Adams*, 192

Adams was prescient about the parades and fireworks, but he was wrong about the date. It was on July 2 that the Second Continental Congress approved the resolution for independence proposed by a delegate from Virginia, Richard Henry Lee, namely, that "these United Colonies are, and of right ought to be, free and independent States, that they are absolved from all allegiance to the British Crown, and that all political connection between them and the State of Great Britain is, and ought to be, totally dissolved." It was the Declaration of Independence that was adopted on July 4. It set forth the reasons for declaring independence from the British King. Contrary to common belief, it was not signed until August 2, and some signatures came later. What we are really celebrating on the Fourth of July is not the act of Independence, but the declaration of it. The ties that bound the colonies to the mother country were severed on July 2. The Second of July is Independence Day; the Fourth of July is Declaration of Independence Day!

What happened in Philadelphia in 1776?

Unfortunately, we do not have the minutes of the Second Continental Congress in 1776, when the members debated the resolution about independence and the Declaration of Independence, because the Congress was acting as a "committee of the whole." All we have are the Journal of the Congress with the final votes and the recollections of some participants many years later, especially Adams and Thomas Jefferson, and they don't often agree! However, according to historians, an important source of information about the proceedings are the notes taken by Jefferson. The subject of independence was only one of many issues confronting the group, as they wrestled with military matters, administrative details and the work of many committees. Jefferson himself was a member of thirty-five different committees.

When Lee first proposed his resolution on independence on June 7, Congress had other business on the agenda and postponed debate until the next day. Resolving itself into a "committee of the whole," the delegates confronted such matters as the fact that some colonies had not received instructions on how to vote, and the possibility of military aid from France or Spain. In the meantime, on June 11 they appointed yet another committee to prepare a list of reasons to justify independence; and on the committee were, besides Jefferson: John Adams, Benjamin Franklin, Roger Sherman, and Robert Livingston. During the month Congress had learned that a large fleet of British ships had sailed into New York harbor and another fleet was poised to attack Charleston, South Carolina. Congress had also learned that the American invasion of Canada had failed.

The first vote on the resolution for independence showed nine colonies in favor, South Carolina and Pennsylvania opposed, Delaware's delegation split, and New York abstaining. However, on July 2, South Carolina changed its vote to "yea," Caesar Rodney returned from a visit to Delaware to break his colony's tie, and Pennsylvania voted in favor because two of its five delegates stayed away. New York's delegates didn't come on board until a week later, but twelve colonies had voted unanimously for Independence on July 2. Jefferson and his committee, appointed to draw up a declaration, reported to the Congress on June 28, but it was tabled while the resolution was debated. The Congress then turned to the Declaration of Independence, debated it for three days, July 2–4, and made many changes in the draft that was presented.

The musical play 1776 was so intriguing because it purported to give a look behind closed doors of what happened during those steamy summer days in the Philadelphia State House, what we now call Independence Hall. The Tony-award-winning musical debuted on Broadway in 1969, was produced as a movie in 1972 with most of the original cast, and has been brought back as an award-winning revival. To achieve dramatic effect, the musical (the book by Peter Stone and music/lyrics by Sherman Edwards) took liberties with the facts and has a number of historical inaccuracies. Most important, the show's creators have combined the two events, the vote on independence and the vote on the Declaration of Independence, with the signing of the document on July 4. Also, the main character, John Adams, is portrayed as "obnoxious," when a leading Adams biographer, David McCullough, claimed that Adams was one of the most respected members of the Congress. Adams used the term, "obnoxious," in his 1805 autobiography after he had suffered through his troubled one-term presidency. Furthermore, the musical portrays Caesar Rodney as an old man about to die, when in fact he was very active in the Revolutionary War after August 2. Of course, Jefferson's wife, Martha, never made the trip to Philadelphia; she was extremely ill, having suffered a miscarriage. Jefferson did not delay in producing a draft because of his violin-playing or many false starts; a draft went to members of the committee in about a week.

Of great importance, the southern delegates did not walk out because of the proposed section in the Declaration on slavery. Other commentators have pointed out that the section was hastily written and most delegates supported its deletion. According to Jefferson's notes, the clause on slavery was left in because the delegates from South Carolina and Georgia were satisfied and wanted to continue the slave trade; the shipping interests of the northern states also profited from slavery. This triangular trade is described in one of the most dramatic songs in the musical, "Molasses to Rum to Slaves," sung by the actor portraying Edward Rutledge of South Carolina.

Why was Independence so long in coming?

American independence was a long time in coming. For years the original thirteen colonies could not agree on anything, let alone independence. Their rivalries and jealousies went deep on such matters as taxes, currency, trade, and commerce. The British Board of Trade, as agents of the monarchy, had ordered an assembly in Albany in 1754 of delegates from the colonies, in order to achieve some unity. In fact, a plan of union was drawn up under the leadership of Benjamin Franklin and approved by the delegates. It would have created an executive branch and a legislature with the power to tax. However, it was rejected by the colonies.

What happened in the next twenty-two years to change the situation and bring about a united declaration of independence? There were at least seven events:

1. The French and Indian War (1755–1763) was the last of a series of wars between the British and the French for the control of the continent. The historian Fred Anderson called it "the war that made America," since the colonies learned to cooperate and the colonists gained a sense of confidence, self-reliance, and military skill. American soldiers in this war who became leaders in the Revolutionary War, besides George Washington, were Israel Putnam, Nathanael Greene, Henry Knox, Peter Schuyler and John Stark.

2. The Stamp Act and other revenue acts, which the British Parliament passed from 1763 on in order to pay the debts from the French and Indian War. These led to organized colonial resistance, riots, protests and assemblies. British efforts to put down the colonial protests led to violent acts such as the "Boston massacre" of 1770. The tax on tea led to the so-called Boston Tea Party of 1773.

3. There were a number of more coercive acts, often called the "Intolerable Acts," such as closing the port of Boston, restricting town meetings, quartering troops in homes, and even the ceding of land north of the Ohio River (the future states of Ohio, Indiana, Illinois) to Canada. This led to the calling of the First Continental Congress in Philadelphia in 1774.

4. In 1775 there were battles between British soldiers and colonials in Lexington, Concord and Bunker (or Breed's) Hill. George Washington was appointed commander of the continental army and took charge of the troops in the Boston area. The British burned Charlestown at the time of the Bunker Hill battle. Later in the year they burned Falmouth, Maine, and Norfolk, Virginia, early in 1776. Despite all of this the Continental Congress still sent petitions to the British Crown and sought to reconcile the colonies with Great Britain. Whatever the disposition of the colonists and their delegates to the Continental Congress, three more events early in 1776 turned the tide.

5. News arrived in the colonies in January 1776, that the King had approved of the "Prohibitory Act," which made colonial shipping and seaports the target of attacks by the British fleet. The British were treating their American cousins as enemy aliens.

6. Copies of the pamphlet *Common Sense* by Thomas Paine began to be circulated in the colonies. Paine, a native of England transplanted to the colonies the previous year, attacked the institution of a hereditary monarchy, called George the Third a "royal brute," and urged immediate independence.

7. Finally, in the spring of 1776 the British government hired thousands of Hessian soldiers and other foreign mercenaries to fight the American colonists. This was the last straw!

It needs to be pointed out that this was not the last straw for many colonists, who remained loyal to the British Empire and were called Loyalists or "Tories." During and after the Revolutionary War they were mistreated by the patriots, and thousands of them left for Canada or elsewhere. Independence was not a sentiment or goal shared by all the inhabitants of the original colonies.

How were the people prepared for Independence?

The people were more prepared for independence than their leaders. In 1765 nine colonies had sent twenty-seven delegates to a Stamp Act Congress in New York City, where a Declaration of Rights and Grievances was passed. As a result of this and many other protests and demonstrations, the Stamp Act was repealed the following year but more onerous taxes and burdens were enacted by the British Parliament.

Earlier, the colonists had protested against a bishop. All of the seven events listed above are in the history books, but there was one more event which is often overlooked or ignored and that was the struggle over the naming of an Anglican bishop for the American colonies. This battle took place in the decades prior to the Revolutionary War and demonstrated the will and determination of the colonists to act in concert regarding what was regarded as an abridgement of their liberties. Non-Anglicans who were predominant in the middle and northern colonies would never consent to the establishment of the Bishopric because it would mean more consolidated power of the Crown and the established Church of England. These new Americans had not forgotten what their ancestors had suffered under earlier bishops and archbishops, which led to the "Great Migration" of Puritans over the ocean to the new world. Anglicans in the southern colonies were also opposed because it would threaten the control of local vestries over the clergy who were called to serve the parishes. Adams later recalled that this fear of an Anglican Bishop aroused the attention of the common people of the colonies to the great power that the British Parliament wielded.

In spite of the fact that Independence was a long time coming, many American colonists had yearned for change for years. John Adams wrote a letter in 1818 to Hezekiah Niles, in which he said that revolution was in the minds and hearts of the people; as well as a change in their sense of duties and obligations, before the Revolutionary War. Much has been written about the emergence of a distinctive American character with traits that set it apart from the old world. Many factors contributed to this new personality: the immigrant experience of pulling up roots and leaving one's native land and family; separation from it by a great ocean; the rigors of survival in an untamed wilderness; the existence of Native Americans whose culture was so different, warfare so cruel, and whose land was being taken from them; the presence of many African-Americans who had been taken against their will, carted over the ocean in the brutal "middle passage," and sold into chattel slavery; the local control over institutions, whether civil or religious. These new Americans were self-reliant, independent, and egalitarian in their ways.

It is true that the colonies had a difficult time agreeing on matters of economic and political policy, but the people had much in common. They were predominantly Protestant in religious background; in fact, it has been estimated that three-fourths of the population were of the Reformed branch of Protestant Christianity, descendants of the Puritans: Congregationalists, Presbyterians, Dutch and German Reformed, French Huguenot, Baptist, Quaker. As latter-day followers of John Calvin, they believed, some with reservations, in the sovereignty of God, the sinfulness of humankind, the place of the "elect," and the virtue of hard work. Even those who were not of Reformed background were greatly influenced by the Puritan ethic. These folk were not satisfied to live in quietism, but were activists in seeking to make a better life for themselves and their children.

These people also found a sense of identity because of the "Great Awakening," a revival of religious enthusiasm which began with Jonathan Edwards in Northampton, Massachusetts, in the 1730s and spread throughout the colonies. It has been said that the awakenings served to lower barriers between the colonies and prepared the way for greater unity. Many of the colonists heard the preaching of the great English evangelist, George Whitefield, on one of his seven trips to the colonies, beginning in 1738. Whitefield became the best-known figure at the time, almost a kind of a "rock star," with thousands flocking to see and hear him wherever he went. Even the worldly Benjamin Franklin, who had left behind his Puritan upbringing, was impressed.

There was also the influence of "Election Sermons." One should not underestimate the power of the pulpit in the colonial period. Clergy were called upon to preach at the regular Fast and Thanksgiving days that were proclaimed and, especially in New England, on Election Days when town officials and magistrates were gathered. These colonial preachers helped to prepare the way for revolution by talking about "no taxation without representation" and resistance to tyrants or unjust rulers. These sermons were often printed and given to members of the colonial assemblies and distributed widely in the colonies.

Finally, the original thirteen colonies were already accustomed to self-government. It is true that the governors of the colonies were appointed by the British Crown, except for Connecticut and Rhode Island, but the people elected members of the colonial assemblies as well as town officials and other magistrates. One of the reasons that Parliament is never mentioned by name in the Declaration of Independence is that the colonists did not accept the rule of Parliament over them. After all, they had their own assemblies, as well as newspapers, committees of correspondence, and other means of communicating throughout the colonies.

What is the Declaration of Independence?

There have been many books on the Declaration of Independence through the years. Two classic studies in the twentieth century were done by Carl Becker, professor of history at Cornell University, and Pauline Maier, professor of American history at M.I.T. Becker had originally been asked to write a small volume on the Declaration as a work of literature, but the project changed so he enlarged it to be a study of its political philosophy, as well as its literary qualities. The result was *The Declaration of Independence: A Study in the History of Political Ideas*, originally published in 1922, reprinted in 1942 and still available today. Becker devoted many pages to the natural rights philosophy and the historical antecedents of the Declaration as well as to what happened to that philosophy in the nineteenth century. According to him, any book on the Declaration "should contain some account of the changes made in the original text and the reasons for making them." In examining the literary qualities, he concluded that the Declaration had the virtue of simplicity, clarity, and logical order.

Pauline Maier's book, *American Scripture: Making the Declaration of Independence* was published in 1997 fully seventy-five years later. She acknowledged her debt to and appreciation for Becker, but added: "In a sense, I have written the book Becker was criticized for not writing," namely seeing the Declaration "as the culmination of a series of revolutionary activities." [3] Maier disagreed with Becker on the main purpose of the Declaration; she felt that it was to set forth the reasons for severing ties with Great Britain and that this was not subordinate to a major premise about natural rights.

Among many other books written about the events leading to the American Revolution and independence from Great Britain, a new one published in 2013 needs to be considered. The author was Richard R. Beeman, professor at the University of Pennsylvania, who expressed appreciation to Pauline Maier, not only for her writings but for her critical appraisal of his new book. Entitled *Our Lives, Our Fortunes and Our Sacred Honor:*

3. Maier, *American Scripture*, xvii, xviii

The Forging of American Independence, 1774–1776, this volume devoted the last three chapters of twenty-five to the actual debate over independence and the Declaration. Its virtue, however, lay in establishing the historical context of the debate in the sessions of the First Continental Congress, which met from September 1774 in Carpenters Hall in Philadelphia and the Second Continental Congress, which convened in May 1775 in the Pennsylvania State House.

A list of what the Declaration is not—and what it is—would be a helpful way of answering the main question:

1. It is not a divine decree, a gift from God or the product of divine inspiration, like tablets of stone on a mountain. Since 1952 the original Declaration has been exhibited in a shrine-like setting in the rotunda of the National Archives in Washington, DC, like some kind of sacred relic behind an altar to be approached with awe and reverence. Instead, the Declaration is a very human creation by an assembly of fallible human beings making political decisions and compromises in a statehouse. These delegates to the Second Continental Congress may have been among the "best and brightest" of the colonies, but they were men filled with fear and frustration, passion and prejudice, and they were very aware that what they were doing was treasonable because of their rebellion against the King of Great Britain and they could all be hung for it.

2. It is not the work of only one man, but the creation of a committee. Becker and Maier, along with other scholars, have examined the changes in the document as it went through three stages: a draft by Jefferson, a committee report, and the final document adopted by the Congress on July 4. Using detective work, these literary sleuths have tried to show the changes made by Jefferson himself, by Adams and Franklin, and by the entire assembly. Almost one fourth of the original text was eliminated. The consensus is that the document was shortened and improved over the original, and is a shining example of how a literary piece can be edited by a committee. Jefferson was not happy with the changes, but he still showed pride of ownership and authorship. For his tombstone Jefferson directed that his first accomplishment listed should be "Author of the Declaration of Independence;" he did not want it mentioned that he was a President of the United States!

3. It did not appear out of the blue as a stroke of genius without precedent. It is the direct descendant of the 1215 Magna Carta and of the 1689 British *Declaration of Right* or *Bill of Rights*, which followed the ouster of King James II, and set forth the rights of the people and the Parliament. The writings of John Locke, English philosopher and essayist, were very familiar in the American colonies. In justifying the "Glorious Revolution" of 1688, Locke wrote about the natural rights of people, which were older than governments. Locke had written that since people were by Nature free, equal, and independent, their consent was needed before being deprived of liberty or property. Quotes from Locke appeared in election sermons and other colonial writings, and form the basis of other declarations, such as the 1775 "Declaration on Taking Up Arms," for which Jefferson had also written the draft. When Jefferson sat down in June 1776 to begin the writing of the Declaration of Independence, he had access to all these precedents, in addition to the draft preamble for the Virginia constitution that he had just written and a copy of George Mason's version of the Virginia Declaration of Rights.

4. It came as no surprise to the American people, but was the culmination of many years of unhappiness with the tyrannical control of the British government. Maier has pointed out that in the previous months there were at least ninety resolutions or instructions about independence that had been adopted up and down the East coast by towns, counties, associations, colonial assemblies, and even three grand juries. She devoted an entire chapter to the "other" declarations of independence and has listed them in Appendix A of her book. Maier has reminded us that only a portion of the colonists took part in these exercises, but they were remarkable in their similarities and in their strong call for independence.

5. It is not a religious statement, but a political document setting forth the reasons for separation of the colonies from the mother country. An entire body of literature has been produced intending to show that the United States was founded on Christian principles and values. Because the U.S. Constitution has been labeled "godless," having no mention of God and including a strict prohibition of any religious test for public office, some have looked to the Declaration of Independence and its references to God as verification of their beliefs and support for their notion of the United States as a "Christian nation." Actually, there

are two different concepts of God in the Declaration: the beginning reflects Jefferson's notions of a more deistic "watchmaker," ("Nature's God" and "Creator"), while at the end members of Congress added more traditional references to God as "Supreme Judge of the World" and "Reliance on the Protection of divine Providence." This is a God who is active in human history. The final document included a kind of "lowest-common-denominator" religion, that would meet the approval of a diverse Congress consisting of Anglicans, Presbyterians, Congregationalists, Deists, agnostics, and a Roman Catholic. To debate whether the Declaration is Christian or un-Christian is a totally misplaced argument.

6. It is not a statement about freedom from government, but freedom from the British government. Soon after the Declaration was approved, a committee was formed to draw up the outlines of a government for the newly independent states. Arguments over the nature of this government have continued through the entire history of this country. Ranged against each other have been the proponents of a strong central government, like Alexander Hamilton, and those who believe that "the best government is the one that governs least." Until the Civil War it was believed that the United States was a federation of sovereign states which could secede at will. The New England states considered leaving the republic at the 1812 Hartford Convention, and in the 1830s South Carolina felt that it could nullify the actions of the federal government. Eleven southern states did secede from the Union after the election of Abraham Lincoln to form a new country, the Confederate States of America. One of the results of the Civil War was to cement the foundation of a united nation with a strong central government and rights and laws that applied to all the citizens of that nation.

7. It is not an historical artifact, but a living charter of American freedom. In its first twenty-five years of life the Declaration was ignored; it was dusted off by Jefferson's own political party during his presidency. In succeeding generations it has become a great rallying cry for those seeking greater freedom in this country and for people and countries all over the world. William Lloyd Garrison and the abolitionist movement appealed to the Declaration and proclaimed that the grievances it listed were pitiful in comparison with the sufferings of slaves. According to Pauline Maier, Abraham Lincoln was provoked by the

attacks on the Declaration by John C. Calhoun and others, like Rufus Choate of Massachusetts, who called the Declaration's natural rights "glittering and sounding generalities." On his way to Washington, DC, for his inauguration as President, Lincoln stopped in Philadelphia and spoke at Independence Hall:

> "I have never had a feeling politically that did not spring from the sentiments embodied in the Declaration of Independence . . . It was not the mere matter of the separation of the colonies from the motherland; but that sentiment in the Declaration of Independence which gave liberty, not alone to the people of this country, but, I hope to the world for all future time. It was that which gave promise that in due time the weight would be lifted from the shoulders of all men."[4]

In 1963 Martin Luther King, Jr., on the steps of the Lincoln Memorial, called on America to "rise up and live out the true meaning of its creed, 'we hold these truths to be self-evident: that all men are created equal.'"

How was the Declaration of Independence celebrated?

According to the Philadelphia newspaper, the Declaration of Independence was read publicly for the first time on July 8 outside the State House to a small crowd. Muskets were shot and bells were rung, but probably not what is called the Liberty Bell, since the rickety wooden steeple of the State House would have collapsed. The bell had been originally commissioned in 1751 to celebrate the fiftieth anniversary of William Penn's Charter of Privileges, Pennsylvania's first constitution. Since fifty years was declared the year of jubilee in the Bible, the bell was inscribed with a verse from Leviticus establishing the jubilee, "proclaim liberty throughout the land unto all the inhabitants thereof." The bell wasn't called the Liberty Bell until the 1830s, when it was adopted by the abolitionist movement as its symbol.

Independence Day wasn't established as a federal holiday until 1941, but annual celebrations of the day go back to the beginning of the country. The first anniversary was celebrated on July 4, 1777, in Philadelphia, with a band playing music, illumination of houses with candles in the windows and fireworks, including a rocket for each of the thirteen states. According to Maier, the *Philadelphia Evening Post* reported: "Thus may the fourth of

---

4. Lincoln, *Speeches and Writings*, 2:213

July, that glorious and ever memorable day, be celebrated through America, by the sons of freedom from age to age till time shall be no more. Amen and amen."[5] The custom was picked up in other places. For example, the town of Bristol, Rhode Island, takes pride in having the oldest Fourth of July celebrations, going back to 1785. Apparently the first observance was organized by the local Congregational minister and consisted of prayers and orations. The Fourth of July oration became the most common way to celebrate, although fireworks grew in popularity during the nineteenth century. My mother bought a copy of one collection of Fourth of July orations, 1786–1861, entitled *Trumpets of Glory*, edited by Henry A. Hawken for the Salmon Brook Historical Society in Granby, Connecticut, as a part of the American Revolution Bicentennial in 1976. Included in the volume were speeches by Daniel Webster, John Quincy Adams, Henry David Thoreau, and even Davy Crockett.

Even before independence had been declared, there were those who felt left out. On March 31, 1776, Abigail Adams wrote a letter to her husband, John, in Philadelphia:

> " . . . I desire you would remember the ladies and be more gener-
> ous and favorable to them than your ancestors. Do not put such
> unlimited power into the hands of the husbands. Remember, all
> men would be tyrants if they could. If particular care and attention
> are not paid to the ladies, we are determined to foment a revolu-
> tion and will not hold ourselves bound to obey any laws in which
> we have no voice or representation."[6]

Seventy-two years later, in 1848, Elizabeth Cady Stanton and Lucretia Mott convened a conference on women's rights in Seneca Falls, and their Declaration of Sentiments" was modeled after the Declaration of Independence: "We hold these truths to be self-evident that all men *and women* are created equal." They pointed out that "the history of mankind is a history of repeated injuries and usurpations on the part of man toward woman." In the long list of grievances they listed such things as being denied the right to vote, the ownership of property, the right to earn a living, access to a thorough education, ordination to the ministry, and representation in the halls of legislation. Sixty-eight women and thirty-two men signed the Declaration. It was another seventy-two years before an amendment went into effect giving women the right to vote.

5. Maier, Ibid, 161
6. Shuffelton, Ibid., 148

William Lloyd Garrison used the occasion of the Fourth of July in 1829 to make his first major public statement against slavery in an oration at the Park Street Church in Boston. Two years later he founded the weekly anti-slavery newspaper, *The Liberator*, and in the next two years started the New England Anti-Slavery Society and, with colleagues, the American Anti-Slavery Society. Frederick Douglass, the African-American slave-turned-freedman, gave a Fourth of July oration in Rochester, NY, in 1852, in which he said:

> "What to the American slave is your Fourth of July? I answer, a day that reveals to him more than all other days of the year the gross injustice and cruelty to which he is the constant victim. To him your celebration is a sham; your boasted liberty an unholy license; your national greatness, your sound of rejoicing are empty and heartless; your denunciation of tyrants, brass-fronted impudence; your shouts of liberty and equality, hollow mockery; your prayers and hymns, your sermons and thanksgivings, with all your religious parades and solemnity, are to him mere bombast, fraud, deception, impiety, and hypocrisy—a thin veil to cover up crimes which would disgrace a nation of savages."[7]

The Thirteenth Amendment to the U.S. Constitution, abolishing slavery, was adopted in 1865. This was followed by the Fourteenth Amendment regarding citizenship rights in 1868, and the Fifteenth Amendment in 1870, namely that voting rights shall not be denied or abridged "on account of race, color, or previous condition of servitude."

For the 100th anniversary in 1876, a Centennial International Exposition was held in Philadelphia on 285 acres of land on West Fairmount Park. More than two hundred buildings were constructed with displays from twenty-six states and eleven countries, marking it as the country's first world fair. The main purpose was to exhibit the country's progress in arts, manufacture, agriculture, and mining; displayed for the first time were Alexander Graham Bell's telephone, the Remington typewriter, Heinz ketchup, and Hires root beer. One of the features was an exhibit of the right arm and torch of the Statue of Liberty, and money charged for admission to climb the ladder to the balcony was used to help finance the rest of the statue. U.S. President Ulysses Grant and his wife attended the opening ceremony in May, and when it closed in November it had registered over ten million in attendance.

7. Douglass, *Oration*, (July 5, 1852) 20

As the 200th anniversary of the Declaration approached, it was decided not to plan a large national exposition or world's fair, like the one in Philadelphia in 1876, but to encourage hundreds and thousands of state and national organizations and local towns and cities to plan Bicentennial events. Coordinating the effort was the American Revolution Bicentennial Administration under the direction of John Warner, former Secretary of the Navy and a future U.S. Senator from Virginia. Activities were organized around three themes: Heritage '76, to remember, reenact and restore the past; Festival USA, to celebrate through dance, drama, music and the arts; and Horizons '76, to plan projects of improvement for the future. Local communities developed programs, applied for grants, and were given recognition with a special Bicentennial flag, with a logo of a white five-point star inside a stylized star of red, white and blue, surrounded by the words, "American Revolution Bicentennial 1776–1976." As President at the time, Gerald R. Ford reminded his fellow citizens of the famous letter of John Adams in 1776 to his wife regarding the kinds of celebrations of the event, but cautioned them about handing down this magnificent experiment in self-government to future generations, free and strong.

The Interchurch Center of New York City created Project FORWARD '76 as an enterprise to strengthen religious participation in the Bicentennial. This project, along with Protestant, Catholic, and Jewish groups produced publications, discussion guides, forums and conferences in order to deal with the important issues of liberty and justice and human rights. On July 4, 1976, Religious Heritage of America brought religious and government leaders together on the steps of the Lincoln Memorial in a worship service that was intended to unite God and country. From a counter-cultural background, Jeremy Rifkin founded the People's Bicentennial Commission to keep front and center the concerns of people, women, African-Americans, Native Americans and others, who had not fully shared in all the fruits of freedom and independence for the 200 years. The People's Commission led a march to the steps of the capitol building to declare independence from big business and big government, with the help of Jane Fonda, Tom Hayden, Dr. Benjamin Spock, and other veterans of the counter-cultural movement of the 1960s.

Conclusion

We need the annual celebration of Independence Day to help us recall our beginnings as a nation and to rededicate ourselves to those principles on which it was founded: that all persons are created equal; that they are endowed with certain unalienable rights, life, liberty, and the pursuit of happiness; that governments are instituted to secure those rights, deriving their just powers from the consent of the governed; that whenever governmental systems become destructive of those ends it is the right of the people to alter or abolish them and institute a new government. These principles, of course, are embodied in the Declaration of Independence. Yet, a group of young people in Indianapolis typed up copies of those statements and asked people at a shopping mall if they would agree to them and sign their names. Very few people did; many people did not agree with the statements and called them Communist, subversive, un-American.

Finally, the Declaration of Independence was not just "pure politics" or the affirmation of rights won by human beings; it was the declaration of unalienable rights endowed upon humankind by their Creator. The proclamation and discussion of ideals of freedom and democracy have spiritual implications, not just political ones. Perhaps, John Adams was right after all, that the anniversary of independence will be commemorated as "the day of deliverance, by solemn acts of devotion to God Almighty," as well as by pomp and parade, guns, bells and fireworks. Those acts of devotion may include prayers, orations and the singing of patriotic songs, such as "My country, 'tis of thee," "America the beautiful," and the more recent "God Bless America." But the promise of our founding charter goes far beyond our "templed hills," "fruited plains," and "shining sea" to embrace the aspirations of the people and cultures of all lands.

CHAPTER 6

Toward the Dignity of Labor

LABOR DAY

LABOR DAY HAS BECOME the unofficial end of summer, a time to close the cottage or cabin, to take the last camping trip, or to fire up the grill for a cookout. There was a time when Labor Day was a rare day off for men and women, who often worked six or seven days a week, up to twelve or more hours a day, at less than a living wage, in an environment often hazardous to their health. It was also a day on which the working class demonstrated its solidarity in the struggle for shorter hours, higher pay, and better working conditions. It was a day when labor organizations or unions issued proclamations, circulated petitions, and distributed press releases.

Now, people are conflicted about their work and ambivalent about labor unions. Some find their identity in their work, and others find their jobs boring or tedious, but everyone looks forward to the paycheck. Studies have shown that less than half of working people find some sense of satisfaction in their jobs. Studs Terkel of Chicago interviewed over a hundred people in various occupations, and the resulting book was originally published in the 1970s with the title, *Working: People Talk About What They Do All Day and How They Feel About What They Do.* In general, people were looking for meaning in their work. One person wanted it to be a "calling," not just a job. Another person felt that the work was too small for the human spirit.

People appreciated what unions had done, but were reluctant about joining, because of perceptions of corruption, irrelevance or powerlessness. One of the most interesting books was published in 2001 with the provocative title, *From the Folks Who Brought You the Weekend: A Short, Illustrated*

History of Labor in the United States. The authors made the case that significant advances in American labor were brought about by organized unions, including the forty-hour week; the minimum wage; free weekends; abolition of child labor; better working conditions; collective bargaining, the rise of the middle class. The book chronicled the successes and failures, the steps forward and backward in the long struggle for workers' rights in the history of the country. In 2012 television's History Channel ran a series of programs on "The Men Who Made America," focusing on the careers of John D. Rockefeller, Andrew Carnegie, and J.P. Morgan, who controlled oil, steel and banking. A program could have been done on the millions of men and women who toiled in the mines and mills, farms and factories, fields and forests, railroads and canals, and elsewhere, to make America what it is.

Yet, throughout American history there has been opposition to labor unions: they have been vilified, and the rights of workers to organize have been attacked. The narrative is one of boom and bust, strikes and strike-breakers, slaves and indentured servants, sit-ins and lockouts, bringing new labor into the country, and outsourcing it elsewhere. Currently, the labor movement is in crisis.

Part of the broadcast of a Bill Moyers television show in 2012 was devoted to the question, "Is labor a lost cause?" It was pointed out that the percentage of union membership among American workers has decreased in sixty years from thirty-five to twelve percent, that there are sixteen million union members, and that membership in public sector unions has exceeded those in the private sector, with the National Education Association the largest, with three million members. Even public sector unions are taking a beating, as state legislatures enact "right-to-work-laws," or otherwise act to limit or control their bargaining rights and other benefits. Corporate profits are at an all-time high, yet wages have been stagnant for years, unemployment remains a persistent problem, and job security is almost non-existent.

Labor Day doesn't quite fit among the "holy days" of American civil religion. It does not celebrate or recognize an event or person in American history shaping our understanding of who we are as a people and our destiny as a nation in the world. It became an official federal holiday in 1894 when President Grover Cleveland sought to appease the labor movement which had suffered a major defeat. In 1894 to quell a strike against the Pullman Company which had resulted in the shut-down of many railroad lines, Cleveland sent federal troops and marshals into Chicago. Twenty-five workers were killed and much damage was done to railroad property. In order to make peace with labor, Cleveland pushed a bill through the U.S. Congress in a matter of weeks to make Labor Day a federal holiday on the first Monday of September.

The roots of Labor Day, however, go back to 1882, when the Central Labor Union in New York City sponsored a "labor holiday" parade on the first Tuesday of September in place of a day of work. Much of the credit went to Matthew Maguire, a machinist from Paterson, New Jersey, and Peter McGuire of New York City, who co-founded the United Brotherhood of Carpenters and Joiners and also the organization which later became the American Federation of Labor. Parades on Labor Day became annual events, and marchers carried signs calling for "8 hours for work, 8 hours for sleep, 8 hours for what we will."

It is important to differentiate the American Labor Day from the International Workers Day, observed in many countries on May 1st. At the 1889 Congress of the Socialist Second International in Paris a decision was made for a day of protest the following May. Despite the fact that the date in May commemorated the Haymarket Affair in Chicago six years earlier, the International Workers Day never caught on in the United States, primarily because of the May Day's strong socialist orientation and because the September Labor Day became so popular among Americans. The 1864 founding of the socialist First International in London was under the leadership of none other than Karl Marx and Friedrich Engels, authors of the *Communist Manifesto.*

The movement for an eight-hour work day became a great rallying cry, as did the push for a five-day work week, and Labor Day street parades demonstrated "the strength and esprit de corps of the trade and labor organization." The day was changed to the first Monday of September in 1884 and was called the "workingman's holiday." In 1887 Oregon created the first state holiday to honor the workers, and seven other states followed suit before the end of the decade.

In the interest of full disclosure, this story has become a very personal one, since both my mother and dad were engaged in child labor as young teenagers. My mother had to quit school by age thirteen and go to work in a factory in order to earn a little money for her family. Through scholarship aid, she was able to go back to school and eventually became a pioneering medical doctor. My dad had lost both his parents before he was seven years old and was brought up by other relatives. He went to work in a lumber camp and in construction, but was also able to go back to school to become a skilled carpenter, later joining the AFL Carpenters Union.

Studies of the Labor Movement

Thousands of studies have been done on the labor movement in this country. Some works have surveyed the entire history, while others have looked at specific organizations, discrete periods of time and places, issues, labor disputes and strikes, disasters in coal mines and factories, or individual labor leaders.

A one-volume study was written by Paul Le Blanc, most recently at LaRoche College, with the title, *A Short History of the United States Working Class: From* Colonial *Times to the 21st Century.* Another history was written by Melvyn Dubofsky, State University of New York at Binghamton; his book has gone through numerous editions, *Labor in America: A History.* The co-author was Foster R. Dulles of Ohio State University. Also, there is the aforementioned *From the Folks Who Brought You the Weekend*, written by Priscilla Murolo, Sarah Lawrence College, and A.B. Chitty, librarian at Queens College, New York. This volume is unique because of the "dramatic cartoon narratives" by Joe Sacco, an acclaimed artist.

A more recent survey was *There is Power in a Union: The Epic Story of Labor in America* by Philip Dray, a free-lance writer in Brooklyn, NY. Dray began his study, not in the colonial period, but in the beginning of the Industrial Revolution in the textile mills of New England in the 1820s. His book told the story of the struggle between capital and labor, pointing out that the original opposition to labor organizations was because of the English system of common law, which considered illegal what were called conspiratorial combinations. In 1842 the supreme court of Massachusetts held that labor unions had the right to exist. The author was concerned that the names of prominent labor leaders were being lost to history and that their stories needed to be told.

Among the issues researched has been the struggle of women in the workplace and their efforts to eke out a livelihood in an environment that was often demeaning and condescending. Not to be overlooked is *We Were There: The Story of Working Women in America* by Barbara Mayer Wertheimer, who was on the extension faculty of Cornell University's School of Industrial and Labor Relations. In the Preface, the author stated "that the story of working women has rarely been included in history books."[1] Other books have documented the plight of African-Americans, both in and out of slavery, as well as children, immigrants, and minorities.

Specific labor disputes and strikes have commanded a great deal of attention. A recent book looked again at the conflict in Chicago in 1886, *Death in the Haymarket: A Story of Chicago, the First Labor Movement, and the Bombing That Divided Gilded Age America,* by James Green, University of Massachusetts in Boston.

One book has covered the entire twentieth century, *State of the Union: A Century of American Labor,* by Nelson Lichtenstein, professor at the University of California at Santa Barbara. An older volume looked at the two generations after the Civil War, *Bread and Roses: The Struggle of American Labor,* 1865–1915, by Milton Meltzer. Understandably, there have been a number of books on the Great Depression and the New Deal.

The worst mining disaster in American history was at Monongah, West Virginia, in 1907, and this event was researched by Davitt McAteer. Originally it was reported that 362 workers, including children, had lost their lives, but McAteer of the Mine Safety and Health Administration, U.S. Department of Labor, has reported that a better estimate would be close to 500. Many were Italian immigrants, and in 2007 a delegation came from Italy to honor those who had died. The second worst mine disaster was in 1909 in Cherry, Illinois. On the 100th anniversary, two books were written by Steve Stout and Karen Tintori. They reported that there were 259 people killed, including some children as young as ten years old. Many of these miners had come recently from Scotland. As a result of this disaster, mine safety standards were developed, the United Mine Workers rose to prominence, and John L. Lewis emerged as the leader.

On March 25, 1911, the Triangle Shirtwaist Company fire in New York City claimed 146 lives, mostly young immigrant women, and the story has been told by Leon Stein and David Von Drehle. It was pointed out that many died because the exit doors had been locked, fire escapes were flimsy, and the one elevator was inadequate for the top floors of the building. The affair was especially tragic because a strike during the previous year had tried to call attention to the lack of safety in the buildings. As a result of the fire, workers' compensation laws were passed, and new workplace safety regulations enacted.

1. Wertheimer, *We Were There,* ix

A rich resource consists of the many biographies and autobiographies of labor leaders. Melvyn Dubofsky and Warren Van Tine of Ohio State University co-edited *Labor Leaders in America*. This book presented the story of fifteen leaders, but it did not include Mary Harris Jones, known as "Mother Jones." This was remedied by a recent biography entitled *Mother Jones: The Most Dangerous Woman in America*, by Elizabeth J. Gorn. (See *Appendix B, Leaders of Labor*.)

Not fitting the above categories was a best-selling book on American history, which has been updated regularly and has gone through many editions. *A People's History of the United States, 1492–Present* by Howard Zinn showed a strong bias for organized labor and its struggles for recognition, a living wage, better and safer working conditions, and other benefits.

Just when it was thought that all the writings of Martin Luther King, Jr. had been published, a new book has appeared, *"All Labor Has Dignity,"* a collection of his speeches at labor union conventions and rallies, which has been edited and introduced by Michael K. Honey, professor at the University of Washington, Tacoma. It has been forgotten that Dr. King was not only the leader of the struggle for civil rights, but also a champion for economic justice, and that he was killed in Memphis, Tennessee, while supporting the strike of that city's sanitation workers.

The Story of American Workers

Organizations for workers go back to the very beginning of the country. A highlight of a parade in Philadelphia celebrating the adoption of the Constitution in 1788 was the participation of hundreds of members of guilds representing the trades and crafts of the city. It is reported that the first strike was in 1768 when tailors in New York City demonstrated against a reduction in their wages. Craft unions grew up in cities in an attempt to maintain prices, set standards for acceptable products, and control employment practices. Cottage industries were the norm, when goods were handmade for domestic consumption or local markets.

Many studies have been done about the beginning of the Industrial Revolution, especially in New England, when work transitioned from home to the factory. Most famous were the textile mills of Lowell and the shoe factories of Lynn, both in Massachusetts. Daughters of farmers in the rural countryside gravitated to Lowell, worked long hours from dawn to dusk, received low wages, lived in company boardinghouses, and followed strict rules. It was reported that by the 1840s there was a movement to reduce the work week to sixty hours and increase the pay to ten cents an hour! Capitalism grew because of these atrocious practices. There were earlier "turnouts" or strikes by these workers in 1834 and 1836.

This early period of American history was characterized by many local trade and craft unions; the first unions in the 1790s included the shoemakers of Philadelphia, the tailors of Baltimore, and the printers and cabinet makers of New York City. The primary purpose of unions was protective, to advance workers' interests, but they were also fraternal. In 1866 the National Labor Union was organized with an eight-hour work day as a goal. It was led by William Sylvis, who also founded the Iron Molders Union of North America. In 1869 the Knights of Labor had its beginnings in Philadelphia as a secret society of garment workers, and it was led by Terence Powderly. The first major national strike was in 1877 against the railroads, with over 100,000 workers involved. However, this strike was not led by a union, but was the result of spontaneous outbursts of frustration by poor and unemployed workers, beginning in Martinsburg, West Virginia, and spreading to Pittsburgh, Chicago, and St. Louis. Federal troops were called in to restore order, much damage was done, and a number of people were killed.

The rise of national unions paralleled the emergence of large corporations and the acquisition of great wealth by a few individuals in what has been called the "gilded age." This period not only saw the creation of great fortunes but the growth of monopolies in oil, steel, railroads by Rockefeller, Carnegie, Jay Gould, and J.P. Morgan. By 1890 the richest one percent of Americans had accumulated a total amount of assets which exceeded the combined total of the poorest fifty percent. In 1896 these wealthy individuals were able to buy the presidency of the United States for William McKinley, according to the 2012 History Channel television series. They were devastated when an anarchist's bullet killed McKinley and brought Theodore Roosevelt into the White House. Teddy Roosevelt called them "malefactors of great wealth;" others called them "robber barons."

This was a difficult time for the labor movement. Periods of economic depression seem to come every decade, which meant that workers were laid off or received pay cuts. And that was the plight of the male native-born workers! Women, African-Americans, and immigrants were at the bottom of the ladder and had a difficult time finding a place in the unions. In addition, courts gave rulings, and legislatures passed laws that outlawed strikes and even the formation of unions. After the decline of the Knights of Labor in the late 1880s, the American Federation of Labor took its place, Founded in 1886 in Columbus, Ohio, it consisted of thirteen national craft unions made up of highly skilled workers.

There was a nation-wide strike in 1886 for an eight-hour day. In Chicago police fired at pickets at the McCormick Reaper Works and killed at least four workers. A protest meeting was held at Haymarket Square on May 4, and when the crowd was dispersing a bomb went off that killed seven policemen and wounded many more. Eight anarchists were arrested and brought to trial in what was called the "crime of the century." All eight persons were convicted, and four were hanged at the gallows, although there was never any proof given as to who threw the bomb, and some of those convicted were not even at the rally. The event was a major setback for the labor movement, and it took years to recover.

A major confrontation between capital and labor occurred in 1892 at Carnegie's steel mill in Homestead, Pennsylvania. Carnegie wanted no union and had turned the management over to Henry Clay Frick. Wages were cut by an average of twenty-two percent, and the union went on strike. Frick closed the mill and hired the Pinkerton Detective Agency to bring in "scabs" or strike-breaking workers. Ten people were killed in an armed battle, and the governor ordered the militia to protect the company, not the workers. Finally, the Carnegie mills were sold to J.P. Morgan and became U.S. Steel, which went at least two generations without a union.

George Pullman, who designed the sleeping car and parlor car for the railroads, developed what was called a model community south of Chicago called Pullman, Illinois. Workers lived in company houses and had their rent and utility bills subtracted from their paychecks. In 1894 there was a downturn in manufacturing, and the wages were cut substantially, but with no change in rent and utility bills. Management received no decrease in their salaries, and dividends remained the same for the shareholders. Members of the American Railway Union, led by Eugene Debs, sought to bring the matter to arbitration, but Pullman refused any kind of compromise. As a result, the railroads were shut down, railroad cars and tracks were destroyed, federal troops and marshals were called in, and at least twenty-five people were killed.

The early twentieth century was characterized by the activity of the National Association of Manufacturers to fight organized labor, the growth of the American Federation of Labor under Samuel Gompers, the beginnings of the Socialist Party led by Eugene Debs, and the emergence of the Industrial Workers of the World with "Big Bill" Haywood at the helm. In 1915 Ralph Chaplin wrote a song, "Solidarity Forever," for the IWW, but it became an anthem of the labor movement. It was sung to the tune of "John Brown's Body," and has been recorded by Pete Seeger and other artists. It is still sung at union meetings and also in other countries such as Canada and Australia. Two of the verses were:

"When the union's inspiration through the workers' blood shall run,
There can be no power greater anywhere beneath the sun;
Yet what force on earth is weaker than the feeble strength of one,
But the union makes us strong.
It is we who plowed the prairies; built the cities where they trade;
Dug the mines and built the workshops, endless miles of railroad laid;
Now we stand outcast and starving midst the wonders we have made;
But the union makes us strong.
Solidarity forever, Solidarity forever, Solidarity forever,
For the union makes us strong."[2]

The Industrial Workers of the World led a large strike in 1912 against the textile manufacturers in Lawrence, Massachusetts. It was reported that workers and their families were in poverty and near-starvation, and yet the company decided to cut their wages. This was the last straw, since a number of grievances had already piled up, so 20,000 workers, primarily women, went on strike. They formed a long picket line extending around the factories and, despite being clubbed by policemen, arrested and harassed, they continued for nearly eleven weeks. Elizabeth Gurley Flynn and "Big Bill" Haywood met with the strikers, and relief was provided. The strikers won a victory, and a remarkable feature of the movement was the singing of songs like "The Internationale," and "Bread and Roses" by James Oppenheim:

"As we come marching, marching, unnumbered women dead
Go crying through our singing their ancient song of bread,
Small art and love and beauty their drudging spirits knew,
Yes, it is bread we fight for, But we fight for roses, too."[3]

2. *The Little Red Song Book*, 92
3. *Ibid*, 17

In the midst of militant labor agitation and violent clashes during this period, one stands out; it was called the "Ludlow massacre." The United Mine Workers had started a strike against mines in Colorado owned by John D. Rockefeller. Eleven thousand strikers and their families had left the mining camps and established tent communities, and the labor advocate called "Mother Jones" came to their support. Militiamen and company guards assisted scab workers, and on April 20, 1914, the militia and guards fired machine guns and burned the tents at Ludlow, killing twenty-one people, including eleven children. As a result, the U.S. Congress passed the Clayton Act, which gave some protection to miners and their right to strike.

During the Progressive Era there was some headway in the movements to eliminate child labor and improve working conditions, but World War I intervened. The 1920s saw both the boom and decline of the labor movement. One problem was the increasing mechanization of labor, and another was the fact that the government supported corporations by reducing taxes, eliminating regulations, increasing protective tariffs, and using muscle and influence to promote international markets. The U.S. Supreme Court ruled that minimum wage laws were unconstitutional. The Great Depression pulled the rug out from under both corporations and labor unions. Over a third of the working people of the country were unemployed.

With the election of Franklin Delano Roosevelt in 1932 and the institution of the "New Deal," the fortunes of labor began to improve. The National Labor Relations Board was created in 1934, and the Wagner Act of 1935 gave unions the right to organize and protected them in many ways. It was made clear that nothing in the act would change the right to strike. However, the Act exempted agricultural, hospital, and domestic workers. Other programs which benefitted workers were also passed, such as Social Security, the Tennessee Valley Authority, the Works Progress Administration, and the Civilian Conservation Corps. John L. Lewis and others established the Congress of Industrial Organizations in 1935, pulling away from the AFL. In 1937 there was a successful sit-down strike at the GM plant in Flint, Michigan. The Fair Labor Standards Act was passed in 1938, setting a minimum wage of twenty-five cents an hour, to be increased to forty cents in two years. Also, the forty-four-hour week was established, with time and a half for overtime, and the prohibition of the employment of children under sixteen years of age.

Despite all the measures and programs, the Great Depression did not really end until the Second World War, which sent millions to fight overseas and created a booming industrial economy. The employment of a large number of women has been dramatized in song and story. After the war the Wagner Act was weakened by the Taft-Hartley Act. Among other things, it made possible the passage of "right to work" laws. In the decades following, there were many other changes in the labor movement: for example, the peak year of membership in unions was 1954; the AFL and the CIO merged in 1955, and the combined membership embraced twenty-four percent of the entire labor force.

Civil rights and anti-war movements in the 1960s impacted workers, followed by the environmental and feminist movements. Those excluded by the Wagner Act began to organize. One of the best examples was the National Farm Workers Association founded by Cesar Chavez and Dolores Huerta in 1962. In 1970 the Occupational Safety and Health Administration (OSHA) was established by the U.S. Congress. Also, in the 1970s there was the expansion of unions into the public sector, a trend which resulted in their union membership exceeding that in the private sector.

However, the decades of the 1980s and 1990s were very difficult ones for labor, and this contributed to the problems in the twenty-first century. The Reagan administration was not friendly to labor. In 1981 the Professional Air Traffic Controllers Organization went on strike, and within forty-eight hours most were fired when they did not return to work. There were tax cuts for corporations, and many industries were de-regulated. The NLRB ruled against unions many times. This period saw many job reductions, plant closing, concessions, and plants moving to Mexico and elsewhere, affecting entire communities. Employment grew in service industries, but lost in agriculture, mining, and manufacturing. The adoption of the North American Fair Trade Agreement (NAFTA) in the 1990s resulted in the loss of an estimated 200,000 jobs.

At the beginning of the twenty-first century it was clear that large multi-national corporations had become more powerful and richer than many countries. It was the era of globalization, with China taking the lead in the manufacturing of goods, with textile industries in Bangladesh, Thailand, and other countries replacing those that used to be in the United States. Wages remained stagnant, but the ratio of CEO pay to that of workers grew astronomically, in the decade of the 1990s from 84 times the workers' wage to 475 times. This means that for a worker making $20,000 a year, his or her corporate CEO would be making $9,500,000. If the end of the nineteenth century was the "gilded age," the early twenty-first century might be called the "diamond-encrusted age."

There were problems in the labor unions, including corruption, financial mismanagement, questionable elections, controversial mergers, and jurisdictional disputes. Commentators have pointed out that unions were bureaucratic entities that were preserving the status quo rather than working for economic and social justice. It took years to recover from the Great Recession of 2008, which caused an increase in unemployment, home foreclosures, bank failures, and bankruptcies. Measures were passed to help the banks, auto industry and other sectors of the economy, but unemployment remained a problem.

Conclusion

Jack Welch, former CEO of General Electric, was quoted as saying that he would like to put factories on a barge and move them to wherever labor was cheapest. The history of labor in the United States is filled with the efforts by capital to find cheap labor and the struggle of working men and women to earn a living wage. In accord with classical laissez faire economics of supply and demand, labor has been treated as a commodity, a cost factor, to keep the bottom line as profitable as possible for owners and shareholders. Human beings have been treated as cogs in a machine rather than as persons with values and ambitions, dreams and aspirations.

Religious institutions have reminded us that people are "children of God," made in the image and likeness of God, sacred, never-to-be-repeated personalities with a heart and a soul. One of the important events in the religious history of this country was the social gospel movement, which sought to apply religious and moral principles to industrial society. In spite of the many issues facing the country at the end of the nineteenth century, it was the "labor question" which commanded the most attention. Washington Gladden is considered the father of the movement. As a Congregational minister in Springfield, Massachusetts, in 1876 he defended the right of laboring people to organize and to strike. Rabbi Stephen S. Wise of the Free Synagogue in New York City, was greatly inspired by Gladden and was a speaker at a rally after the Triangle Shirtwaist Co. fire of 1911. He called for penitence and action, recognizing that the disaster could have been prevented and calling for safety standards and measures to protect working people.

Churches responded to the plight of workers in different ways. A number of Protestant denominations established agencies to deal with the labor issue. The Federal Council of Churches began its work in 1908 and issued a social creed, which called for the abolition of child labor, regulation of the conditions of toil for women, protection from disease and accident, a living wage, and old age assistance. Soon after the First World War the National Catholic Welfare Council was founded, with John A. Ryan in charge of its social action department. He became an advisor to President Roosevelt as the "New Deal" was developed.

On a personal note, I preached at the Cherry Congregational Church in Illinois in 1959 on the fiftieth anniversary of the Cherry Mine Disaster, and called attention to the work of Graham Taylor of the Chicago Theological Seminary, who had come to Bureau County and led funeral services for some of the victims. Taylor pioneered in the field of social ethics, which was carried on by his successors Arthur Holt and Vic Obenhaus.

The American Federation of Labor adopted a resolution to make the Sunday before Labor Day a special day dedicated to the spiritual and educational aspects of the labor movement. With the cooperation of the Federal Council of Churches, sermons and other resources were made available for use. When it seemed that the social gospel movement had ceased, along came Martin Luther King. Jr., to give new life to it. To the striking sanitation workers in Memphis on March 18, 1968, he said:

> "You are demanding that this city will respect the dignity of labor. So often we overlook the work and the significance of those who are not in professional jobs, of those who are not in the so-called big jobs. But let me say to you tonight, that whenever you are engaged in work that serves humanity and is for the building of humanity, it has dignity and it has worth."[4]

It has been said that there is as much dignity in a worker's lunch pail as in a briefcase.

Howard Zinn has written that the U.S. Constitution was designed for the aggrandizement of the wealthy elite at the expense of the poor. However, constitutional provisions for the sanctity of contracts, the right to levy taxes, and the Fourteenth Amendment guarantee of no deprivation of life, liberty and property without due process, do not in themselves disenfranchise people. President Lincoln said it best when he declared that

4. Honey, ed., *All Labor Has Dignity*, 171

the founding documents of this country were designed to safeguard equal opportunity for advancement.

Some leaders of labor erred when they tried to change the American economic system to a form of socialism, and did not expound enough on the founding documents of the country. Some leaders of industry erred in not recognizing labor unions and failing to develop partnerships with them in profit-sharing and other programs for their mutual advantage. Both labor and industry erred in using violent methods to resolve conflicts. Unfortunately, working people have had to resort to violence in order to be heard.

Maybe Labor Day does belong in the "holy days" of American civil religion after all. It does not honor one individual or one event that shaped the country, but rather the millions of working men and women and their leaders, who made the country what it is, who have toiled long hours at poor pay to make something of themselves, to get ahead, to make a better future for their children, to pursue what has been called the American dream. It honors the many thousands who lost their lives in accidents, fires, labor conflicts, and mine disasters. It honors those who were created equal and endowed by their creator with certain unalienable rights, life, liberty, and the pursuit of happiness. It honors those who have struggled through the generations to embody and activate the rights of freedom of speech, the press, assembly, and to petition for redress of grievances.

In a Labor Day greeting in 1904 Eugene Debs wrote: "Labor Day is a good day to rest the hands and give the brain a chance—to think about what has been, and is, and is yet to be. The workingman is the only man in whose presence I take off my hat. As I salute him, I honor myself."[5]

---

5. Debs, *DEBS: His Life, Writings, and Speeches*, 289–90

CHAPTER 7

The Blessings of Liberty

CONSTITUTION DAY AND CITIZENSHIP DAY, SEPTEMBER 17

CONSTITUTION DAY IS NOT a federal holiday, but it should be celebrated each year as the culmination of one of the greatest events in human history. When the thirty-nine delegates lined up to sign the new Constitution for the United States of America on September 17, 1787, in Philadelphia, they were ushering in a new age, when people would govern themselves without kings or emperors and decide how much power to delegate to others. This Constitution not only established the framework for the most stable, successful democratic republic in world history, but it also provided a model for other countries around the world.

This new nation was fortunate to have in Philadelphia that fateful summer four remarkable leaders, who would have risen to the top in any assembly because of their talent and wisdom: George Washington, Alexander Hamilton, James Madison, and Benjamin Franklin. (Thomas Jefferson and John Adams were serving overseas as envoys.) Indeed, in the twenty-first century when some people are fearful of "elites" in government, it is well to remember that the Constitution was created by some of the best educated and experienced men of the original thirteen states, including governors, congressmen, judges, lawyers, civic and business leaders, and even some trained in medicine and theology. In the twenty-first century, when political parties are polarized and government faces gridlock, it is good to be reminded that these delegates in Philadelphia arrived at mutual interests, found a way to reconcile their differences and agreed on compromises which saved the Convention and designed a structure, however flawed, that has stood the test of time.

The Convention met between May and September 1787, including some of the hottest summer days, and the delegates could not open the windows of the Old State House for fear that their secret negotiations would be imperiled, but they also wanted to keep the flies out. There were fifty-five delegates in Philadelphia that summer, but some left early; some came late, like the two delegates from New Hampshire; and others were sporadic in their attendance, like Hamilton; and one state, Rhode Island, did not send any delegates at all. The Confederation Congress was meeting at the same time in New York City and some men were delegates to both. There were three delegates who stayed with the Convention until the end and then refused to add their signatures to the document. What the Convention achieved was not only the foundation for a government, but a process for amending it and a procedure for ratifying assemblies in each of the states. The debates in the states were fueled by the papers and arguments of those opposed to the Constitution and a series of eighty-five essays by James Madison, Alexander Hamilton, and John Jay in favor of the Constitution called the *Federalist Papers*. When the ninth and tenth states, New Hampshire and Virginia, had ratified the Constitution by June 1788, it went into effect.

There was a great celebration throughout the states in the summer of 1788, but especially in Philadelphia, birthplace of the country, on Independence Day, July 4. Bells rang, ships shot their cannons, and a parade, called the "Grand Federal Procession," moved through the streets of the city. There were bands and military units, floats representing each of the states, and one for the "federal edifice" and one for the signing of the Constitution. People of various occupations and guilds marched on foot. There were architects and carpenters, farmers and weavers, artisans and laborers, brewers and bakers and candlestick makers, and clergy of all denominations. The ship, *Union*, was mounted on a carriage and was drawn through the streets by horses with its entire crew on board. The parade ended with a lavish picnic, where ten toasts were drunk to everyone from George Washington to the signers and the states. By evening, it was said, 17,000 celebrants "soberly" returned to their homes.

On the Bicentennial of the signing of the Constitution, September 17, 1987, the city of Philadelphia pulled out all the stops and recreated the grand parade, the "Federal Procession," with bands, military units, floats, and people of many occupations, making their way down Benjamin Franklin Parkway, past the City Hall with the statue of William Penn on top, and down Market Street. There was a ceremony at Independence Hall, at which President Ronald Reagan addressed the crowd, saying: "If our Constitution has endured, through times perilous as well as prosperous, it has not been simply as a plan of government, no matter how ingenious or inspired that might be. This document that we honor today has always been something more to us, filled with a deeper feeling than one of simple admiration—a feeling, one might say, more of reverence."[1] In the evening there was a gala, celebrity-laden event at the old Civic Center, hosted by Warren E. Burger, former Chief Justice of the U.S. Supreme Court and chairman of the Commission on the Bicentennial of the U.S. Constitution. The commission itself had authorized commemorative coins and souvenirs, including the "We the people" banners, and had reported on Bicentennial activities throughout the country.

The Bicentennial of the Constitution was celebrated all year with a variety of programs, projects, and publications. One was a series of lectures at Baylor University in Waco, Texas, by Gordon S. Wood, professor at Brown University, who later won the Pulitzer Prize for history in 1993 with his book, *The Radicalism of the American Republic*. Entitled "The Making of the Constitution," Wood's lectures discussed the problems with both the Articles of Confederation and with the various state legislatures, which led to the calling of the Constitutional Convention in 1787. Regarding the delegates, he concluded that "despite the myths, they were not demi-gods and the Constitution was not a miracle." The Constitution was "without doubt a monumental political act, but it did not solve many of the political problems its creators expected to solve."[2]

Thurgood Marshall, a Justice of the U.S. Supreme Court, was more critical. In his reflections on the Bicentennial on May 6, 1987, Marshall wrote regarding the delegates that "the government they devised was defective from the start, requiring several amendments, a civil war, and momentous social transformation to attain the system of constitutional government, . . . that we hold as fundamental today." Marshall concluded by saying that he would celebrate the Bicentennial of the Constitution "as

1. Reagan, Address at Independence Hall, September 17, 1987
2. Wood, G. "The Making of the Constitution," 36

a living document, including the Bill of Rights and the other amendments protecting individual freedoms and human rights."[3]

Constitution Day is a more recent addition to the American patriotic calendar. The newspaper publisher William Randolph Hearst had recommended in 1939 that there be an American Citizenship Day, and the U.S. Congress voted the following year to establish "I am an American Day," to be observed on the third Sunday of May. In 1952 a law was passed changing it to "Citizenship Day," a day that was used in various places for the naturalization ceremony for new citizens of the country. Then in 1956 the Congress asked the President to proclaim "Constitution Week" from September 17 to 23. The last change was made in 2004 when September 17 was designated as "Constitution Day and Citizenship Day." It was also voted that those educational institutions receiving federal funds should have an educational program each year on the Constitution.

Creation of the Constitution

Both George Washington and James Madison felt that a miracle had occurred in Philadelphia in 1787. This was expressed by Washington in a letter to the Marquis de Lafayette, and by Madison in a letter to Thomas Jefferson. In her 1966 book Catherine Drinker Bowen, an award-winning biographer, chose the title, *Miracle at Philadelphia: The Story of the Constitutional Convention, May to September* 1787, to tell the dramatic story. Her book was called a classic and was reprinted in 1986 in time for the Bicentennial of the Constitution with a Foreword by Warren E. Burger. He called it "a singular work of narrative history" and the "best single popular book" on the subject. Bowen discovered that, unlike the Continental Congress of 1776 which produced the Declaration of Independence, there was an extensive record of what was said and done in Philadelphia the summer of 1787.

Bowen lifted the curtain on this historic drama and made us all witnesses. Through her work we know the personalities of the delegates, hear their voices as they addressed the chair, George Washington, or each other. She kept us in suspense at the end of June, when the Convention was in danger of breaking up for lack of agreement, and in three chapters took us on a "Journey through the American states" and to the "Western Territory."

3. Marshall, "Reflections on the Bicentennial of the Constitution," *Harvard Law Review* 101 (1) 2

She resumed the story with the "Great Compromise" and concluded with two chapters on the ratification of the Constitution.

Since the 1960s other writers have tried their hand at telling the story. Even before Bowen's book there was a popular work, *The Birthday of the Constitution: An Informal History*, written in 1964 by Donald Barr Chidsey. At the same time as Bowen, in 1966, there was published *1787: The Grand Convention*, by Clinton Rossiter, professor at Cornell University. Another professor, Richard B. Morris of Columbia University, wrote *Witnesses at the Creation: Hamilton, Madison, Jay, and the Constitution* in 1985. As the title suggested, his attention was focused on the three leaders who wrote the *Federalist Papers*, one of whom, John Jay, was not even a delegate to the Convention.

Published a year before the Bicentennial was *Decision in Philadelphia: The Constitutional Convention of 1787*, written in 1986 by Christopher Collier, the Connecticut state historian, and his brother, James Lincoln Collier. Also in time for the Bicentennial year of 1987 was *A More Perfect Union: The Making of the United States Constitution* by William Peters, a producer of TV and film documentaries and director of Yale University Films.

In 2002 a book, *A Brilliant Solution: Inventing the American Constitution,* was written by Carol Berkin, professor at Baruch College and the Graduate Center of the City University of New York. Another book, *The Summer of 1787: The Men Who Invented the Constitution,* was written in 2007 by David O Stewart, an attorney in Washington, DC. His focus was on the four men who should be regarded as the "Fathers of the Constitution:" James Madison of Virginia, who formulated the Virginia Plan; James Wilson of Pennsylvania, a vocal proponent of a strong national government; John Rutledge of South Carolina, who chaired the Committee of Detail and upheld the interests of the southern states; and Gouverneur Morris of Pennsylvania, who chaired the Committee of Style, wrote the Preamble, and put the Constitution in its final form.

A more recent book was *Plain, Honest Men: The Making of the American Constitution*, published in 2009 and written by Richard R. Beeman, professor at the University of Pennsylvania. Beeman took the title of his book from a quote of Gouverneur Morris, who said about the Constitution: that it was not a work from Heaven, but the work of "plain, honest men."

What these authors share in common is an understanding of the failures of the Articles of Confederation, which had been drawn up in 1777 but not ratified until 1781. The limited government established by the Articles gave no power to the national legislature to raise and levy taxes, create an army, regulate trade and commerce, and negotiate treaties. It was a "league of friendship" among sovereign states, and any decision by the congress required unanimous consent by the thirteen states, each one with one vote. Virginia and Maryland quarreled over the use of the Potomac River, Rhode Island charged tolls on its portion of the Post Road, and the paper currency issued by the states was "not worth a continental." The new nation was in danger of splitting up into two or three confederations.

In addition, it was humiliated by foreign governments: Great Britain did not remove its forts from the northwestern frontier; Spain controlled shipping on the Mississippi River; Barbary pirates attacked American ships in the Mediterranean; and there were raids on Georgia from Spanish Florida. In 1781 there was the discontent of Revolutionary War officers, who had not received their pay and benefits, and a possible insurrection was averted by General Washington himself in Newburgh, NY. In late 1786 and early 1787 hundreds of debtor farmers, led by Daniel Shays, protested the foreclosures of their farms. They closed down courthouses in western Massachusetts and attacked the armory in Springfield in the bitter winter.

James Madison, George Washington, and Alexander Hamilton were aware of the desperate situation. Through the Virginia legislature a national convention was called to be held in Annapolis in 1786, but only five states were represented. Another convention was convened in Philadelphia in 1787 with the sole purpose of amending the Articles of Confederation. Madison came early to Philadelphia with an entirely new government, which was called the "Virginia Plan." After a week of the Convention the delegates voted that "a national government ought to be established, consisting of a supreme legislature, judiciary, and executive." Madison wanted the legislature to be elected on a proportional basis. This plan formed the basis for debate at the Convention. It was countered by the New Jersey Plan, submitted by William Paterson of New Jersey, which would continue the formula of equal representation by each state. Alexander Hamilton proposed his own plan, which would effectively reduce the power of the states, provide for an upper house and executive elected for life, and have state governors appointed by the national legislature. This plan was considered so extreme that it was not even debated, but it served to give more credibility to Madison's moderate plan for a stronger central government.

In addition to the battle between "large states" and "small states" over representation, the subject of slavery created controversy. If slavery had been restricted or abolished by the new Constitution, it was understood that the southern delegates would have walked out. John Rutledge negotiated a compromise that preserved the "peculiar institution" of the southern states and protected the shipping interests of the northern states. Another important compromise, credited to Roger Sherman of Connecticut, was to give the lower house representation proportionate to population, and to the upper house the same number of votes for each state. By late July a Committee of Detail was appointed to prepare a working Constitution that would embody all the agreements and compromises. This was followed the next month by a Committee of Style and Arrangement, which would produce the final document. It was at this time that the chairman, Gouverneur Morris, wrote a Preamble beginning with the words, "We the people," rather than "We the states of New Hampshire, Massachusetts, etc." The document was revised some more and then signed on September 17, 1787, by thirty-nine delegates.

Ratification

During the next eleven months, from September to the following August, the American people were engaged in the most extensive debate in political philosophy ever undertaken by a country. In her book, *Ratification: The People Debate the Constitution, 1787–1788*, Pauline Maier, professor at MIT, has told the story with a sense of suspense, as if it had just happened. The new Constitution was printed in its entirety in newspapers throughout the states, and before the month of September was over some critical essays also appeared attacking the plan as "un-republican," "aristocratic," and designed "to deprive us of our liberties." Bowen had pointed out in her book that "it is much easier to alarm people than to inform them." Critics used names like Cato and Brutus from the Roman republic to identify their essays, so Hamilton, Madison, and John Jay collaborated in writing eighty-five essays with the pseudonym of Publius, a founder of the ancient Roman republic. These essays were published in New York newspapers between October 1787 and the following March, and were reprinted in two volumes in March and May 1788. This collection of essays is available today as "The Federalist Papers," which has been called "the most important work in political science that has ever been written, or is likely ever to be written in the United States."[4]

4. Rossiter, ed. *Federalist Papers*, ix

It would be hard to summarize the reasons for opposing the Constitution. There was a concern about the powers given to the new national government. It was recognized that these powers were ostensibly limited, but they extended to everything of importance, especially the power to levy and collect taxes. It was felt that the "necessary and proper" clause might be interpreted to give the new Congress complete power over the state governments. Taken together with the Preamble, this clause could give Congress the right to make laws at its own discretion. In addition, the power to raise a standing army was considered dangerous to liberty.

There were other objections to the Constitution. The granting of supreme judicial power could subvert the courts of the states, could extend the legislative and executive power of the federal government, and could ultimately destroy the authority of the states. The Supreme Court would become more powerful than the other branches of government and would be subject to no control. It was also felt that representative government could not exist in a country so large, with so many diverse interests and regions. There was also a strong feeling that the new Constitution lacked a Bill of Rights, and there was a sentiment that the three/fifths proportional representation of slaves was unreasonable and unjust.

With the exception of Rhode Island, the states called for the election of delegates to ratifying conventions. On December 6th Delaware became the first state to ratify the Constitution and did it unanimously. New Jersey followed with a unanimous vote. The large state of Pennsylvania voted in favor on December 12th with a vote of 46 to 23. Georgia and Connecticut voted in favor on January 2nd, Georgia unanimously and Connecticut by a vote of 128 to 42. The issue was much more contentious in Massachusetts, but it finally passed on February 5th by a vote of 187 to 168. Maryland passed it 63 to 11 and South Carolina 149 to 46. New Hampshire had met in February and then postponed a decision to June 21st, when it finally voted in favor 57 to 46. This was the ninth state to ratify, thereby placing the Constitution into effect. Virginia's vote on June 25th was close, 89 to 79, while in New York it almost lost, finally winning on July 26th by a vote of 30 to 27. North Carolina was the one state to reject the plan by a vote of 184 to 83, but both North Carolina and Rhode Island joined the Union the following year when the government had already been established and Washington was serving his first term as President.

Flaws in the Original Constitution

On the last day of the Convention before the Constitution was signed, Benjamin Franklin was reported to have said that there were "several parts of this Constitution which I do not at present approve." He added: "I agree to this Constitution with all its faults, if they are such, because I think a general government necessary for us . . . I doubt too whether any other Convention we can obtain may be able to make a better Constitution." There were other delegates who had problems with it; even James Madison was disappointed because some of the things he had proposed were not approved. In the last of the Federalist Papers, No. 85, Hamilton dealt with those who felt that the Constitution was not perfect. He wrote: "I never expect to see a perfect work from imperfect man." There were many flaws in the original Constitution, but most of them have been corrected or resolved.

Foremost, there was the lack of a Bill of Rights. George Mason of Virginia, author of that state's Declaration of Rights, brought the subject up at the Convention in early September, but it was felt that it was unnecessary since the state constitutions contained a list of rights and the new federal Constitution would not conflict with them. The first Congress under the leadership of Madison submitted twelve amendments to the states for ratification and ten were accepted in 1791, becoming the Bill of Rights.

The policies and procedures for the national government were laid out in the Constitution, but not the rights and privileges of ordinary Americans. This is why the Fourteenth Amendment, ratified in 1868, was one of the most important, since it extended the rights in the first ten amendments to all citizens. It declared that all persons born or naturalized in the United States were citizens, and that they could not be deprived of life, liberty, or property without due process of law, nor could they be deprived of the equal protection of the laws.

A major flaw was the acceptance of slavery. For purposes of apportioning representatives to the House, each slave was counted as three-fifths of a person. This ratio, like so many other provisions, was a compromise between southern delegates who wanted slaves fully counted so as to increase the number of their Congressmen, and other delegates who felt that slaves should not be counted at all because they were regarded as property; why not count horses and cattle? But that was not all. The new Constitution explicitly allowed the slave trade to continue until 1808, and it also instituted a provision for the return of fugitive slaves. All this was done without even using the word "slaves." It took a Civil War and the Thirteenth Amendment, ratified in 1865, before slavery and involuntary servitude were abolished.

The inclusion of a social issue like slavery in the original Constitution could have set a precedent for other matters which do not belong in the blueprint for a government. Fortunately, in the history of the country there was only one other social policy added, and that was the prohibition of alcoholic beverages in the Eighteenth Amendment adopted in 1919. This was repealed in 1933 by the Twenty-First Amendment. There has been no lack of subjects or special interests for inclusion in the Constitution, including prayer in the schools, marriage, flag-burning, right to life, balanced budget and a "Christian Amendment."

Article II Section Two had a very awkward plan for electing the President and Vice President, and this was one of the first problems to be corrected, when the Twelfth Amendment was ratified in 1804. However this did not eliminate the Electoral College, which made it possible for a President to be elected while not winning the popular vote. This has happened four times in American history, in 1876, 1888, 2000, and 2016. Unfortunately, the Electoral College still exists.

There was considerable attention given to how the President was to be elected, but little to the powers and responsibilities of the chief magistrate. It may have been assumed that everybody knew what an executive officer does, but it was George Washington in his two terms as the first President who established precedents for the high office that have continued to the present day.

The original Constitution called for U.S. Senators to be elected by the state legislatures, which was a way of placating the states and assuring them direct input in maintaining a federal system. This was changed by the Seventeenth Amendment, ratified in 1913, which provided for the direct election of Senators by the people.

There was uncertainty in the Constitution about the power of the Supreme Court, since Article III was not clear on the subject. In an 1803 case, Marbury v. Madison, the Supreme Court, under Chief Justice John Marshall, settled the matter once and for all. The Supreme Court had the power to declare unconstitutional acts of Congress. Marshall wrote: "It is emphatically the province and duty of the judicial department to say what the law is . . . a law repugnant to the Constitution is void."

There was ambiguity regarding the power of the national government in relation to the states. The delegates in Philadelphia had wanted an "energetic" government, one that would meet every exigency, but that was not possible. They ended up with a list of eighteen powers of Congress in Article I, Section Eight, and a list of what states could not do in Section Ten. In the case of McCulloch v. Maryland in 1819 the U.S. Supreme Court decided unanimously that Congress had the right to charter a national bank, even though it was not listed among the eighteen powers. The Court declared that the eighteenth power in Section Eight gave Congress the right to make laws which shall be "necessary and proper" for carrying out its purposes.

Another ambiguity had to do with the matter of war. The Constitution made the President the Commander in Chief of the armed forces, but gave the power to declare war to the Congress, without clarifying what would happen if the nation was attacked while Congress was not in session. This was finally cleared up in 1973 by the War Power Resolution.

Strange as it may seem, the Constitution did not give people the right to vote or to have their votes counted. It is true that when the Constitution was adopted, many states had property or religious qualifications for voting, and they were not interfered with. The Constitution has not been changed in that regard, except to grant African-Americans the right to vote by the Fifteenth Amendment (1870), and women by the Nineteenth Amendment (1920); the poll tax and other taxes were removed by the Twenty-fourth Amendment (1964), and 18 year olds were given the right to vote by the Twenty-sixth Amendment (1971).

Another flaw in the Constitution was the lack of any limitation for a term of office. After Franklin Delano Roosevelt had been elected four times as President, there was a movement to restrict the chief executive to two terms in office, and the Twenty-second Amendment was ratified in 1951 to accomplish that. However, there still is no restriction on the number of terms for members of Congress.

The Colliers in their book, *Decision in Philadelphia: The Constitutional Convention of 1787*, have made the claim that designating the Vice President as the President of the Senate and able to vote in the case of a tie, is a breach of the important rule of separation of powers and a mixing of the executive and legislative branches of government. This has never been changed, and people look upon it as the only constitutionally mandated function of a Vice President, unless the President cannot serve because of death, disability or removal.

Actually, the Constitution was not clear regarding the replacement of the President. The Twenty-fifth Amendment, ratified in 1967, finally cleared up this matter and established the process for deciding on the inability of the President to discharge the powers and duties of that office.

The Constitution is Not a Religious Document

The Constitution has been called a "godly" instrument which reflects the "Christian principles upon which the country was founded." The leader of one church declared that the delegates in Philadelphia were inspired by God. There is a constant refrain in American public life that the country has lost its way, that government is too big, that its values have been subverted, and that a return to its constitutional principles is necessary to save the country from what are perceived to be "godless," "humanistic," or "secular" forces. The country is considered by many to be a "Christian nation," not so much because the majority of its citizens may be adherents of that religious tradition, but because the Constitution laid the foundation for it.

It is true that the delegates in Philadelphia came from a variety of Christian denominations or backgrounds, including several Roman Catholics. It is true that they represented a continuum of religious beliefs, from deistic or more rational world views to more orthodox Christian viewpoints. It is true that Thomas Jefferson, when he saw the list of the delegates to the convention, called them "demi-gods." However, these delegates were hard-nosed, pragmatic, political or civic leaders who were sent to Philadelphia to find a solution to the dysfunctional and embarrassing confederation and construct a republican form of government which would unite the country and at the same time preserve the liberties won in the recent Revolutionary War. One cannot look to the Constitution for an affirmation or verification of biblical, theological, or religious principles. The Constitution is the political blueprint for the country and its governmental institutions and procedures. It is not a religious document.

In the first place, there is no mention of God in the Constitution, unlike the Declaration of Independence, where there are four references to the deity. It is inaccurate to look upon the Constitution as just a continuation of the Declaration, since they were each designed for totally different purposes. One was to give the reasons for declaring independence from Great Britain, the other to establish the framework for a new nation.

Second, the only mention of religion in the entire document is the prohibition of a religious test for public office. Scholars throughout American history have reminded us that the original Constitution provided for "separation of church and state," even before the First Amendment was adopted.

Third, the records of the Constitutional Convention show no discussion of religion, except to comment briefly and vote unanimously on the "no religious test" in Article VI.

Fourth, Benjamin Franklin proposed the institution of daily prayer when proceedings in the convention seemed difficult, but it was rejected on the basis that such a move would give the impression of failure and, besides there was no money to pay a chaplain. Alexander Hamilton was reported to have said that they did not need the aid of a "foreign power!"

Fifth, there is an entire school of thought, identified with Charles Beard, which has proposed an economic interpretation of the Constitution, since the delegates were consumed with strong interests in preserving and extending slavery, safeguarding shipping interests, dealing with debts and specie, and protecting investments in western lands. It is true that they were concerned about paying off debt, restoring the value of money, fending off foreign encroachment, but they were primarily devoted to creating a government that would work.

Sixth, one of the great constitutional scholars, Clinton Rossiter, has pointed out that religious principles were not proclaimed by the delegates; it was a secular convention intended to provide worldly and temporal solutions to very critical political problems.

Seventh, in the extensive ratification process there was no consideration of religion, except to acknowledge the existence of a multiplicity of religious sects in the country, to call for a Bill of Rights to protect freedom of conscience, and to consider the "no religious test" provision.

Civil and Religious Liberty

In the midst of the debates of the Constitutional Convention Charles Pinckney of South Carolina said: "Our true situation appears to me to be this: a new extensive country containing within itself the materials for forming a government capable of extending to its citizens all the blessings of civil and religious liberty." This sentiment was incorporated in the Preamble of the Constitution:

"We the people of the United States, in order to form a more perfect union, establish justice, insure domestic tranquility, provide
for the common defense, promote the general welfare, and secure
the blessings of liberty to ourselves and our posterity, do ordain
and establish this Constitution for the United States of America."[5]

In effect, this Preamble became the "mission statement" of the new
nation. Even before the Bill of Rights was added, the original Constitution
sought to safeguard the civil and religious liberties of the people.

The people, with limits on suffrage imposed by the states, had the
right to choose their own representatives, and those elected were subject to
accountability and the opportunity to run for re-election every two years.
Other protections were written into the Constitution: the writ of habeas
corpus was maintained, along with trial by jury; there were to be no ex-
post-facto laws or bills of attainder (or no extinction of civil rights and
capacities).

Furthermore, no title of nobility would be given, eliminating the possibility of an aristocracy. The citizens of each state would be entitled to all
the privileges and immunities of citizens in the several states. Civil liberties
were protected by features of the Constitution such as "separation of powers," "checks and balances," and a judicial system with a Supreme Court,
with appellate jurisdiction, and other courts to be established.

As far as religious liberty is concerned, it is made possible by the "separation of church and state." There are those who are critical of this concept,
because it doesn't fit the modern American situation with a multiplicity of
religious groups and many forms of government. There are others who say
that the phrase is not found anywhere in the Constitution, but one could
say that the terms, "supremacy clause," "separation of powers," and "checks
and balances," are nowhere to be found either, but this does not make them
devoid of meaning and power in explaining parts of the Constitution.

This has been an important principle of jurisprudence throughout
American history. For example, in the 1947 case, *Everson v. Board of Education*, the U. S. Supreme Court gave a clear definition of the matter: "Neither
a state nor the Federal Government can set up a church. Neither can pass
laws which aid one religion, aid all religions, or prefer one religion over
another . . . In the words of Jefferson, the clause against establishment of

5. Preamble, *U.S. Constitution*

religion by law was intended to erect 'a wall of separation between Church and State."[6]

This concept of "separation" was in the original Constitution before the First Amendment was adopted. One of the most important essays written in 1987 was by James E. Wood, Jr., editor of the *Journal of Church and State*. It was entitled "No Religious Test Shall Ever Be Required: Reflections on the Bicentennial of the U.S. Constitution." Wood pointed out that the adoption of this prohibition "precluded the possibility of any church-state union or the establishment of a state church in the absence of religious test." He quoted Supreme Court Justice Joseph Story, who wrote regarding the clause: "It had a higher object; to cut off forever every pretense of any alliance between church and state in the national government."[7] This constitutional provision has served, not only to protect religious freedom, but also to enable religious traditions to flourish in this country without government aid or interference.

Conclusion

The delegates at the 1787 Convention in Philadelphia wanted a strong, energetic central government. Rather than revising the Articles of Confederation with its limited government, they devised a plan which has met the needs of a large, growing country in a global community. They gave the Congress power, but it was not unlimited. Eighteen powers were enumerated, but the final one authorized the body to make laws which shall be "necessary and proper" for carrying out its purposes. They also provided for an executive veto and a Supreme Court as restraints when the Congress over-reached its powers. It is misleading to quote Jefferson about government being the best that governs least, because he was not satisfied with the Constitution and wanted the country to remain a simple agrarian society. Thanks to Alexander Hamilton, Washington's first Secretary of the Treasury, a strong foundation was created for economic growth and development, providing for a bank, the extension of credit, and the encouragement of manufacturing. This has been a marvel for the rest of the world.

James Madison said that the new government was both national and federal. It was national because the people and their elected representatives established it, and it reached down to touch the lives of individual citizens.

6. *Everson v. Board of Education*, 330 US I (1947)

7. Wood, J. *Journal of Church and State*, 29: (2) 200

It was federal because the states played an important role, but also with restraints placed upon them. It is a complete misunderstanding to consider the Constitution as a compact among sovereign states, any of which could leave the Union at will. The Constitution began with the words, "We the people," not "We the states."

Regarding the argument whether the Constitution can be interpreted in its "original intent" or as a "living document," Justice Stephen Breyer of the U.S. Supreme Court has written in his book, *Making Our Democracy Work: A Judge's View,* that "the Court should reject approaches to interpreting the Constitution that consider the document's scope and application as fixed at the moment of framing." Rather, "the Court should regard the Constitution as containing unwavering values that must be applied flexibly to ever-changing circumstances."[8] Fortunately, the Constitution provided for two methods of amendment and set in motion a judiciary, both of which have kept the structure up to date and able to deal with circumstances in the post-industrial, electronic/digital age that the delegates could never have imagined.

Even before the Bill of Rights was added in 1791, the Constitution extended the "blessings of liberty," both civil and religious, to all citizens. Safeguards were provided, such as "separation of powers," "checks and balances," limited powers, the amendment process and judicial review. Even before the First Amendment was adopted with its "no establishment" and "free exercise of religion" clauses, there was the unprecedented institution of "separation of church and state," which meant that all religions or no religion were on an equal footing, and religion was allowed to thrive and prosper without government favor or interference. The Constitution was "neutral" in terms of religion. In other words, it did not establish a "Christian nation."

Finally, it has been maintained that the U.S. Constitution was a prime example of God's working in history, in the eternal struggle for freedom and justice for all people. Benjamin Franklin, when he called unsuccessfully for prayer, remembered the daily prayers of the Continental Congress and addressed Washington as he presided over the convention:

> "Our prayers, Sir, were heard, and they were graciously answered. All of us who were engaged in the struggle must have observed frequent instances of superintending providence in our favor. To that kind providence we owe this happy opportunity of consulting

8. Breyer, *Making Our Democracy Work,* 75

in peace on the means of establishing our future national felicity. And have we now forgotten that powerful friend? Or do we imagine that we no longer need his assistance? I have lived, Sir, a long time, and the longer I live, the more convincing proofs I see of this truth—that God governs in the affairs of men. And if a sparrow cannot fall to the ground without his notice, is it probable that an empire can be raised without his aid?"[9]

9. Farrand, ed. *The Records of the Federal Convention,* Vol.1, 451

CHAPTER 8

Admiral of the Ocean Sea

COLUMBUS DAY

"In fourteen hundred and ninety two
Columbus sailed the ocean blue.
He had three ships and left from Spain;
He sailed through sunshine, wind and rain.
He sailed by night; he sailed by day;
He used the stars to find his way."[1]

THIS IS THE BEGINNING of a familiar poem about Columbus, and almost everyone knows the first two lines. The date 1492 is so ingrained on everyone's memory that someone even wrote a spoof poem, claiming that in 1492 George Washington crossed the Delaware, the Pilgrims landed on Plymouth Rock, Barbara Frietchie displayed her country's flag, and Pocahontas saved John Smith's life!

In the beginning of American independence and the early development of this nation, Columbus took on mythic proportions and achieved iconic status as the symbol and ideal of freedom, nationhood, and glory. This new nation rediscovered Columbus and used his name for the new national capital, the District of Columbia; King's College in New York City changed its name to Columbia University; the capital of the new state of Ohio was named Columbus; towns, streets, squares, plazas, and rivers were named after him, and statues of him were dedicated. Phyllis Wheatley, the

---

1. Anonymous, "In fourteen hundred ninety two"

African-American poet, suggested at the time of the American Revolution that the name America be changed to Columbia as a poetic representation of the country, and songs were sung like "Columbia, the Gem of the Ocean." Daniel Webster, in his 1800 Fourth of July oration at Dartmouth College, referred to the name of this country as "Columbia" more often than "America." Even my hometown district in Connecticut was called Columbia at the end of the eighteenth century and would have been incorporated as a town with that name, if one did not already exist in the eastern part of the state. In Canada there is the province of British Columbia, and Colombia is a country in South America.

The name Columbus was so representative of the inventive genius and industrial might of this nation that its world's fair in Chicago on the 400th anniversary of his first landfall was called the Columbian Exposition. Here on the shores of Lake Michigan and along a Midway in 1892–1893 were displayed the technological marvels of a great country about to embark on its own military and naval expansion into the world. In a lagoon were docked the replicas of the *Nina*, the *Pinta*, and the *Santa Maria*. Unique among the features of this fair, along with the first Ferris wheel and other attractions, was the World Parliament of Religions, which brought followers of the eastern religions, Islam, Buddhism, and Hinduism, into contact with the adherents of the religions of Christianity and Judaism. It was the meeting of two worlds and cultures and was a preview of the multi-cultural, multi-ethnic nation of today.

It has been reported that observances of Columbus Day go back to the colonial period of this country. Italian-Americans celebrated the day in New York City in 1866 in recognition of their ethnic and national identity, and other Catholic immigrants to these shores saw the tradition of Columbus Day as a way to coalesce feelings of religious piety and American citizenship. A new lay fraternal organization was founded by Fr. Michael McGivney in New Haven, Connecticut, in 1882 with the name, the Knights of Columbus. A first-generation Italian in Denver, Angelo Noce, lobbied for the cause, and Colorado first decreed Columbus Day as a state holiday in 1905, and it became state law in 1907. In 1934 Columbus Day was declared a federal holiday, and in 1971 the U.S. Congress established it on the second Monday of October.

As the 500th anniversary of Columbus's landfall approached, opposition to its celebration grew. Native Americans grew louder in their demonstrations and denunciations, spilling over from protests at Plymouth

Rock of anniversaries of the Pilgrims landing, as well as at the settlement at Jamestown. In 1990 Native Americans from both continents gathered in Quito, Ecuador, to organize a resistance movement, and this was followed by a meeting in Davis, California. October 12, 1992, was declared an "International Day of Solidarity with Indigenous People." The United Nations, after a few years of debate, decided not to promote a 500th anniversary of the Columbus voyage. The National Council of Churches declared that because of "genocide, slavery, ecocide, and exploitation" following Columbus, it should be a day of penitence, not celebration. One denomination, the United Church of Christ, changed the day on its calendar to "Indigenous Peoples' Day." The National Conference of Catholic Bishops recognized the "harsh and painful" treatment of indigenous Americans, but declared it was not a "totally negative experience."

Columbus Day parades were canceled in Los Angeles and elsewhere, and Berkeley, California, changed the name to "Indigenous Peoples Day." Delegates to the 1992 Earth Summit in Rio de Janeiro echoed the concerns about the ill treatment of indigenous people (which is still going on in the Amazon basin and elsewhere) and the ecological devastation that has continued. A statue of Columbus in Haiti was torn down, and more recently one in Caracas, Venezuela, (similar to the dismantling of the statue of Saddam Hussein in Baghdad in the Iraq war). Columbus has been blamed for all the problems which beset the new world he encountered: rape and pillage, slavery and genocide, forced labor and exploitation, despoliation of the land.

Where does that leave us today?

In the twentieth century there were a number of important discoveries, writings and projects about Columbus, which attempted to separate the man from the myth, the sinner from the saint, the legend from the life. This has not been another case of debunking a hero or of revisionist history, but an attempt to interpret the life and legacy of an obscure son of a weaver in Genoa, who signed an agreement with King Ferdinand and Queen Isabella of Spain to become Admiral of the Ocean Sea, Viceroy and Governor of the Indies. Columbus was born around 1451, as far as can be determined, and died in 1506, but a lot happened in his short life between those two dates.

In 1942 there was published the monumental two-volume biography of Columbus with extensive notes, and this was issued also as a 671-page book, *Admiral of the Ocean Sea: A Life of Christopher Columbus*, written by Samuel Eliot Morison, eminent professor of history at Harvard University, experienced sailor, and distinguished Rear Admiral of the U.S. Naval Reserve. He later produced a fifteen-volume history of U.S. naval operations in the Second World War. In addition to using many sources, in 1939, before the outbreak of the war, Morison sailed across the Atlantic Ocean, following the route of Columbus. He had also sailed the Bahamas and Caribbean area in a barentine and a ketch in 1939–40 with the Harvard Columbus Expedition. Morison sought to bring the Italian navigator down to earth and solve all the mysteries about his career, including the controversial issue as to where Columbus first made landfall in the new world. Morison said "without a doubt" that it was Watlings Island in the Bahamas, which Columbus called San Salvador. Morison's conclusion was that Columbus was the greatest navigator of his time, but a poor governor and administrator of the new Spanish settlements.

Among many other books, an outstanding one is *The Mysterious History of Columbus: An Exploration of the Man, the Myth, the Legacy*, written in 1991 by John Noble Wilford, science correspondent for the *New York Times,* who has also been a professor and has won two Pulitzer Prizes for his writing. Although in his own words Wilford has criticized some of Morison's attitudes and conclusions, he has been profoundly influenced and inspired by that careful scholarship and the eloquent literary style. More than any other person, Wilford has pulled together over five centuries of research and writing and has assembled all of the accomplishments and failures, conclusions and controversies surrounding the Admiral of the Ocean Sea.

Also in time for the 500th anniversary in 1992, there was published *The Log of Christopher Columbus*, translated by Robert H. Fuson. This original account of the first voyage in 1492–93 had some gaps filled in by reference to a biography of Columbus by his son, Hernando, and other early sixteenth century accounts. There was also a PBS television series on "Columbus and the Age of Discovery" with a companion book by Zvi Dor-Ner, executive producer of the series and the author of many books. In addition, the National Geographic Society carried out a Columbus Project, which resulted, among other things, in an article in the November 1986 issue of the magazine on "Search for the First Columbus Landfall," written by Joseph Judge, senior associate editor. The project found that the first landfall was at Samana Cay in the Bahamas, not Watlings Island, as concluded by Morison.

Two other studies about Columbus were published in the January 1992 issue of *National Geographic*. The first was an attempt by Eugene Lyon to discover who Columbus was and what motivated him to make the trip over the uncharted Atlantic. Lyon examined the papers and books of the Admiral in the archives of a palace in Madrid and in the library of the cathedral in Seville, both collections surviving for 500 years. Most important among these papers was a copy of a letter from a Florentine geographer, Toscanelli, who described how one could reach the fabled East by sailing West, thereby meeting the Grand Khan, the ruler of China, and finding the riches of the island of Japan. There were other books and papers on which Columbus had made voluminous notes, indicating his acquaintance with the Bible, histories, and geographies. Lyon recounted that Columbus was undergirded by a deep religious faith and believed that "God made me the messenger of the new heaven and the new earth . . . He showed me where to find it."[2] This was the source of Columbus's vision and mission.

By age nineteen Columbus was already learning the ways of the sea, sailing the Mediterranean and at twenty-five was living in Portugal, acquiring skills and knowledge from the school of mariners led by Prince Henry the Navigator. He learned from sailors that the Atlantic was a "Sea of Darkness," full of great darkness, high waters and winds, many storms, and countless monsters. By 1484 Columbus proposed his trip west across the Atlantic to the King of Portugal but it was rejected. It took him seven years to convince the monarchs of Spain to support his expedition, and they finally did after the Moorish rulers had been driven from Granada.

The second study was a report by Kathleen A. Deagan about the excavations of the first Spanish settlement in the New World. On his second voyage Columbus had established a town on the northern shore of Hispaniola (now the Dominican Republic), which he called La Isabela in honor of the Spanish Queen. Teams from the University of Florida and from Venezuela have uncovered remains of a wall and unearthed many artifacts from this colonial site, which lasted only five years. The settlement was a disappointment to the Spaniards because of the lack of gold and because it was plagued with disease and doomed by rebellion and violent reprisals. The town was replaced by Santo Domingo on the southern coast of the island.

2. Lyon, *National Geographic*, 181: (1) 38

A more recent book has been called the first complete portrait of Columbus in over half a century. *Columbus: The Four Voyages* was written by Laurence Bergreen and published in 2011. His volume about the Admiral showed a man of vanity, self-promotion and fortune-seeking, who altered his logs and reports in order to keep others off the track. Bergreen felt that it was impossible to identify the site of Columbus's first landfall.

What are we to believe?

First, Columbus did not discover America. The continents of North and South America were discovered by the original Native Americans thousands of years ago when they first traversed the ice-bound land bridge between Asia and Alaska. The Kon-Tiki expedition showed that it was possible for other peoples to have conquered the oceans and arrived at these shores. As far as Europeans are concerned, there were Vikings and Leif Ericson, who made it to Newfoundland, called "Vinland," 500 years before Columbus. What Columbus did was to begin the so-called "Age of Discovery," the encounter between Europeans and Native Americans, the "re-uniting" of peoples who had been separated by oceans for many millennia. With Columbus the story was being communicated.

Second, Columbus believed until the end of his life that he had found the Indies, the stepping stones to the fabled lands of China and Japan with gold and silver and spices, that had been reported by Marco Polo. The Admiral never believed that he had found a new world, despite the mounting evidence. Certainly, America was not named after him, otherwise we would be known as the United States of Columbia! A navigator who did believe he had discovered a new continent was Amerigo Vespucci, a native of Florence, who apparently had sailed down the coast of South America in 1499–1500. His story reached a group in the village of St. Die in the province of Lorraine, France. They had a printing press and brought out a new geography book with a map on which the illustrator and cartographer, Martin Waldseemuller of southern Germany, had given the new continent the name, "America." Some would say, "the rest is history." Some say Columbus was robbed!

Third, Columbus did have three ships when he sailed from Spain, along with about ninety men and boys, but only two ships made it back across the ocean. On the first voyage they had explored islands in the Bahamas and the northern shores of Cuba and Hispaniola, but on the shore of what is now Haiti his flagship, the *Santa Maria*, was grounded by human error and could not be saved. On Christmas Day, 1492, Columbus established a small settlement called Navidad, and the timbers from the ship were removed to build a fortress. Most of the crew stayed behind when the *Nina* and the *Pinta* sailed back to Spain. On his second voyage, 1493–96, Columbus sailed with a fleet of seventeen ships and over twelve hundred men and boys (all male again!). They explored the Leeward Islands, Puerto Rico, Jamaica, as well as Cuba and Hispaniola. The third voyage in 1498–1500 involved six ships and an undetermined number of persons, and the coasts of South America and Trinidad were explored. It was at the end of this voyage that Columbus was arrested by a chief justice sent by the Spanish monarchs and brought back to Spain in chains. Charges against him were dropped, but his mismanagement of the enterprise had become clear. The fourth and final voyage was carried out in 1502–04 with four ships and 135 males, and the coast of Central America was explored. This time Columbus and two leaking vessels were marooned in Jamaica for a year and had to be rescued.

Fourth, one line of the poem reads: "He used the stars to find his way." Morison has gone into great detail to show that Columbus was a skilled navigator by compass or "dead reckoning." He had learned the art of navigating in Portugal and had traveled west to the Azores and down to Madeira, the Cape Verde Islands and the west coast of Africa as well as north to the British Isles and possibly to Iceland. He became familiar with the trade winds and westerly winds on the Atlantic Ocean. On his voyages to the new world Columbus carried a primitive type of quadrant which used the sun or stars to determine one's position on the sea, but Columbus had trouble with it and even made mistakes in finding the North Star. In spite of these shortcomings, his biographers have praised his knowledge of waves, wind and weather. One time Columbus used an almanac to predict a full eclipse of the moon, which terrified the natives into doing his bidding. At another time his prediction of a imminent hurricane enabled him to find shelter for his ship while an entire fleet of Spanish vessels was lost.

Fifth, his greatest mistake, of course, was his treatment of the Native Americans he encountered and incorrectly labeled as "Indians," because he thought he had reached the Indies. In the log of his first voyage Columbus described these people "as naked as their mothers bore them," unarmed, docile, friendly, and without any religion. It should be pointed out that on the first voyage Columbus ordered his men not to harm the natives and not to touch any of their belongings, even when they went into abandoned huts after the inhabitants had fled. (It was learned later that these native people thought the strange men in their sailing ships had come from heaven.) Unfortunately, even in this first trip he set in motion plans for making them slaves, since they seemed ready to do anything he told them to do.

Columbus did not invent slavery. For centuries Arab traders had trafficked in human beings, and some form of servitude goes back to the dawn of human civilization. The Portuguese, in their subjugation of Africans, built trading posts and fortresses on the west coast of Africa and designed ships with holds below for human cargo. In the 1839 story of the Amistad, when fifty-nine Mendi people were kidnapped from Sierra Leone and taken to Cuba, it was the Portuguese fort and ship that evoked the most fear and terror. Because of the harsh treatment, enslavement, and European-borne diseases the Taino people, whom Columbus first met in 1492, were mostly exterminated by the middle of the next century. The poem has the line: "Indians! Indians! Columbus cried; His heart was filled with joyful pride." But there was no joy for these native people, and the conquistadors who followed continued the process of destruction and decimation. One wonders what would have happened if the Aztec, Inca, and Maya civilizations had been more technologically advanced and first created the ocean-going sailing ships to "discover" and colonize Europe!

Sixth, it is not in the poem, but it is clear that Columbus was a very religious, pious man. He had been influenced and supported by the Franciscans and other religious orders, he observed the Catholic rites and rituals faithfully, and even at sea without benefit of clergy he followed the daily cycle of prayer and holy offices. All hands on deck would say the Pater Noster (Lord's Prayer), the Ave Maria, the Credo, and in the evening would sing "Salve Regina" (Hail, O Queen, mother of mercy). Columbus knew the Bible and quoted from it extensively. The Admiral took his baptized name, Christopher, seriously and considered himself a "Christ-bearer," one called by God to extend the Christian faith to other peoples. Wilford devoted an entire chapter in his book to Columbus as "God's Messenger."

Apparently, after his third voyage Columbus began writing the *Book of Prophecies*, in which he compiled scriptural passages to show his discoveries as a part of God's plan in history, as a way of converting people, and as a proclamation of the divine part in the process. In these pages Columbus professed his belief that his work had fulfilled the prophecies of the Bible as well as those of other ancient writers such as Seneca. In response to the question as to how Columbus could reconcile his Christian faith with his terrible treatment of the natives, part of the answer lies in the prevalent medieval notion of a "just war." It can be argued that the attitude of the Admiral toward the native people changed radically when he returned on his second voyage and discovered that the Spanish fort at Navidad had been destroyed and all the Spaniards killed. These people were not as innocent and defenseless as he believed, and this led to more hostile encounters, especially when the search for gold became all-consuming.

Seventh, another line of the poem is right on target: "Columbus sailed on to find some gold to bring back home, as he'd been told." The search or lust for gold overwhelmed the other objectives, namely to claim lands for the King and Queen of Spain and to convert the natives to the Christian faith. An evangelical Congregational preacher in Canterbury, Connecticut, Philip Jerome Cleveland, explained in the 1940s that the Spaniards came to the new world in search of gold while the Pilgrims came in search of God; one for earthly riches, the other for religious liberty. This may be a little simplified, but the truth of the matter is that the later voyages of Columbus included hundreds of men, not to establish a thriving colony, but to extract as much gold as possible from the rocks, streams, and villagers. There were no women on these ships, only soldiers, sailors, craftsmen, miners, and even appraisers or assayers to determine the value of the precious metals. Some of the natives they encountered wore golden bracelets and other ornaments and readily traded them to the Spaniards for worthless beads and other trinkets. Soon the native population was coerced into finding quotas of gold, with cruel punishments handed out for failure.

Eighth, finally, Columbus did not prove to people that the world was round. Contrary to Washington Irving's early biography and other legends, most people in the fifteenth century did not believe in a flat earth, where ships could fall off the edge of the world. The conflict at that time was over the size of the world and how many thousands of miles separated the continents. Columbus himself believed that if you sailed West over the Atlantic Ocean you would reach the Indies or a part of Asia. He had no idea that North America and South America were standing in the way, plus the much larger Pacific Ocean. That was for Magellan and his crew to discover.

What should we conclude?

Contrary to some accounts, Columbus cannot be regarded as a modern man. He had one foot planted firmly in the Middle Ages and one foot planted firmly in the Renaissance. His main underlying purpose was to find the riches of the Indies in order to finance another medieval crusade to take back the Holy Land from the Islamic invaders and occupiers. It was his dream that Jerusalem and the Holy Sepulcher would be restored to Christian control under a great crusade led by the Spanish monarchs. Another example of his medieval world-view was the establishment of a kind of feudal system in the Caribbean islands. The natives were to serve and labor for their feudal lords in exchange for some kind of protection from their enemies, especially tribes called the Caribs, who were considered cannibalistic. Columbus also reflected his medieval roots in his prophecies and predictions and an apocalyptic notion of the "end times" or eschatology. Every age has used prophetic books and passages in the Bible to predict current events or the end of the world, and Columbus was no exception. According to his estimation, the world would end in 150 years. Christians today, enamored of the *Left Behind* series of books and other apocalyptic tales, can appreciate the mind-set of the great Admiral.

But he was also a man of the Renaissance, with his spirit of adventure and inquiry, his appreciation of the natural world with all its sights and sounds and smells. The story is told about the Renaissance poet, Petrarch, who went up on top of a mountain, not to pray and meditate like the monks of his day, but to admire the view. This was the story of Columbus who wrote in his log about all the wonders of trees and flowers, mountains and waterfalls, rocks and coral, brightly colored fish and parrots, that he encountered in the New World. He was no naturalist and could not identify accurately all that he saw, but this does not diminish his sensitivity to the sights of flora and fauna, the aroma of fruits and flowers, the taste of native foods and fish. It has been said that he inaugurated a "Columbian exchange," as products and people were carried back and forth across the ocean in an early form of global economy.

Why should Columbus Day be observed?

There are at least four reasons.

1. First and foremost, his voyage changed history. His landfall in the Bahamas on October 12, 1492, ushered in the age of discovery (unlike the voyage of Ericson or anyone else). It brought people and continents together, for good or ill; it represented an encounter and

clash of civilizations, a culture shock that electrified the Europeans and spelled the downfall of the Native American way of life. It was as if the people of the so-called civilized world had climbed into a time machine and traveled back to an earlier age on the planet. Indeed, Columbus thought he had discovered the "Garden of Eden," that he had found some kind of terrestrial paradise. This history-changing event can only be compared to Gutenberg's invention of the printing press and Martin Luther's launching of the Reformation. The mentalities of people and the maps of the world were changed forever, and there was no turning back

2. Second, the work of Columbus represents an important contribution by a Roman Catholic to the unfolding of human and American history. Time does not permit a recital of the many outbreaks of virulent anti-Catholicism which have pervaded the American experience. The bias and prejudice against those with a religious loyalty to a "foreign" Pope has been well documented in U.S. history. It did not begin with the French and Indian War, but it was exacerbated by the enlistment of only Protestants in the militias to drive the Catholic power of France from the continent. It can be argued that the election of John F. Kennedy, the first U.S. President who was a Roman Catholic, may have contributed to a more tolerant attitude and a more ecumenical spirit. In 1892 the Knights of Columbus urged Catholic people to celebrate Columbus Day because it was a "Catholic event." However, Columbus transcends all ethnic and national loyalties and religious traditions. Columbus Day is a time for all people to join together in remembrance and reflection, as well as thanksgiving. There is the wonderful story of my mother—a proud descendant of the Pilgrim fathers and mothers and the Huguenots; she placed in honor on her library bookcase not only a replica of the *Mayflower* but also one of the *Santa Maria*.

It should be pointed out that there was a movement afoot in the late nineteenth and early twentieth centuries to urge the Roman Catholic Church to make Columbus a saint. It had the support of the Knights of Columbus, a French Count, and even the Pope, but nothing came of it. The process of canonization did not get off the ground, in part because of Columbus's irregular living arrangements. He had married into Portuguese nobility around 1479; her name was Dona Felipa Perestrello e Moniz. A son Diego was born, but his wife died in 1485. Columbus fell in love with a peasant woman, Beatriz Enriquez de Arana, but they never got married in spite of the mariner's deep religious faith, probably because she was of a lower social standing and he could not present her at the royal court. A son, Ferdinand or Hernando, was born out of wedlock, and he was the one who wrote an early biography of Columbus. Columbus remained devoted to his mistress and provided for her care in his will.

3. The observance of the day is a recognition of the Spanish or Hispanic influence in the formation and development of this country and as a note of solidarity with the other peoples and countries who share this hemisphere. The oldest communities in this country in continuous existence are Santa Fe and St. Augustine, founded by the Spanish. Who can forget Ponce de Leon, de Soto, Coronado and others in the southern and southwestern parts of this nation, or the string of missions throughout California created by Father Juniper Serra? The date of the landing of Columbus is celebrated or observed in many Latin American countries as "Dia de la Raza," or day of the race, the coming together of people from Europe and the Americas. In Venezuela under President Hugo Chavez the name of the festival was changed to "Dia de la Resistencia Indigena" or Day of Indigenous Resistance.

4. Finally, it is a day of religious significance, since Columbus believed that he was led by God to venture out on an unknown ocean, to expand the consciousness of the known world, and to bring new peoples into the fold of the Christian church. In spite of his failures and shortcomings, we can admire his vision, his courage, and his persistence against all odds, in braving the storms at sea and overcoming the fears on board ship, to charter a new course for humankind. Again and again in his log Columbus expressed his thanks to Almighty God for divine providence and care, mercy and grace. If nothing else, the day should be set aside for reflection and repentance, for dialogue as well as debate, for prayer as well as pageantry.

Columbus was representative of an age whose holy scriptures did not encompass life beyond the known world and did not include some peoples and continents in its sacred story. One can appreciate this dilemma fully by realizing that "people of the Book," especially Jews and Christians, may not be prepared today for finding sentient life beyond this planet. Stephen Hawking, the brilliant astrophysicist and professor at Cambridge University, has cautioned human beings in any future encounter with aliens from space. He is reported to have said that a visit by extraterrestrials to earth would be like Columbus coming to the Americas, and we know that did not turn out very well for the Native Americans! What will the discovery of life on other solar systems do to the terra-centric understanding of people, who believed that "God so loved the world," and that we are God's "chosen people," that this is "God's world," and that God created it in the beginning? Are our notions of God too small for the reaches of outer space?

Not only the memory but the legacy of Columbus has been perpetuated by the fantasies and actualities of space exploration. In his 1865 novel *From the Earth to the Moon*, Jules Verne named the vehicle *Columbiad* that was fired from a giant cannon. In our modern era, vehicles for space travel have been also named after Columbus. In the Apollo Eleven space flight, which landed men on the moon for the first time in 1969, the command module was called *Columbia*. Michael Collins operated the module in orbit around the moon, while Neil Armstrong and Buzz Aldrin landed on the moon's surface in the lunar module called *Eagle* ("the *Eagle* has landed"). The first space shuttle to orbit the earth in 1981 was named *Columbia*. It successfully completed twenty-eighth missions, but its twenty-ninth mission resulted in the disintegration of the spacecraft when re-entering earth's atmosphere. All seven members of the crew, along with the spaceship, have been memorialized in many ways, including in an album released in 2008 by Ann Cabrera entitled *Columbia: We Dare to Dream*. This was followed by a song recorded by John Legend, "Dare to Dream." The NASA space program resumed with the launching of *Discovery* in 2005, but *Columbia* will not be forgotten.

Columbus dared to dream! In 1991, long before the *Columbia* disaster, a book was published, *Columbus and the Age of Discovery*. In memory of Columbus and in tribute to those brave astronauts, we quote from the final paragraph of the book, *Columbus and the Age of Discovery* written by Zvi Dor-Ner, as follows:

> "If there is a core of nobility to Columbus, a part of the man uncolored by his deeds and their consequences good or bad, it is the part of him that searched for a new route, a new way. This much we can cherish without qualification; this much can still speak to our romance with adventure and discovery. It is, after all, what moves us in our own search for new ways of knowledge, and what will doubtless continue to lead us into dilemmas of Columbian proportions. Of all the places and things we have named after Columbus, the most fitting of all may be *Columbia*, the shuttle-caravel

that sails from Earth to the dark edges of space, on yet another human quest for knowledge and profit, power and glory."[3]

Conclusion

It may be foolhardy to pen a conclusion after such an inspiring paragraph comparing the space shuttle *Columbia* to the caravel-type sailing ships of Columbus's time. However, the point is a valid one, that there are still frontiers to explore and there is still a pioneering spirit in humankind to venture out into the unknown. Columbus has been a controversial figure; his heroic stature has been challenged by descendants of the indigenous Americans who suffered under his oppressive policies and the descendants of the Africans who were brought to these shores as slaves.

Research, archeological excavation, and attempts to follow his sailing routes have revealed the humanity and skill of the Admiral as a creature of the medieval period of history as well as of the Renaissance. Nevertheless, the facts are indisputable. Whether we call it an "Age of Discovery" or an "age of colonization," the voyages of Columbus brought peoples of the hemispheres together and created a global exchange that far exceeded the silk roads and spice routes that developed after Marco Polo.

There are those who would like to eliminate Columbus Day or change its name, but its observance is critical in recognizing an event that changed history, that was engineered by a deeply religious person of the Catholic faith, and that recognizes the great and growing Hispanic influence in our own country and in our hemisphere. It is an occasion not only for annual parades by Italian-Americans and their cohorts, but a time to bring peoples of all ethnic, racial, and religious backgrounds together, since the Columbus journey was a triumph of the human spirit against insurmountable odds. Most important, it reveals again the guiding providence of God in human history and in the beginning of American history.

In 1951 The Reconstructionist Press in New York City published the book, *The Faith of America: Prayers, Readings, and Songs for the Celebration of American Holidays.* It was compiled by Rabbi Mordecai M. Kaplan, founder of the Reconstructionist movement in Judaism, J. Paul Williams of the Department of Religion at Mt. Holyoke College, and Eugene Kohn,

3. Dor-Ner, *Columbus and the Age of Discovery,* 342

an author and managing editor. In the introduction to the resources for Columbus Day the editors wrote in part:

> "For Columbus to have undertaken that westward journey in the kind of ships available to men in those days was a great act of faith. The notion that the world was round and that one could reach the east by sailing toward the west had indeed been propounded before that time. The arguments were known to Columbus. But no one had yet put the theory to the test. How many well-reasoned theories have foundered on the rocks of hard fact! Columbus had the faith that the results of sound reason would be by experience. He had the courage to express his faith in action, in defiance of dangers both and fancied.
>
> "And God blessed the faith of Columbus by rewarding it with a success beyond his dreams. His voyages uncovered a new continent in which the ancient civilizations of Europe could take root in virgin soil, renew their vigor, and yield a civilization such as the world had not yet known. That is what makes Columbus Day worthy of celebration."[4]

4. Kaplan et al, eds., *The Faith of America*, 221

CHAPTER 9

To Honor Veterans and Dedicate
Ourselves to World Peace

VETERANS DAY

IN THE *MALLARD FILLMORE* comic strip by Bruce Tinsley in the newspaper one Sunday, November 11th, the question was asked of Mallard, "What's the difference between Veterans Day and Memorial Day?" The answer was: "Some of the heroes we honor on Veterans Day . . . we can still thank in person." In the last frame there is a note from the cartoonist to his father, thanking him for all that he did in the Second World War to keep the world free. An asterisk indicated that his father served on the USS *San Jacinto* in the South Pacific.

On the day after this cartoon appeared, when Veterans Day was officially observed, there appeared in the *New York Times* an op-ed piece by Richard Rubin, "Over There—And Gone Forever," which told the story of the last living veteran of the First World War who actually served in Europe, 106-year-old Frank Buckles of West Virginia. According to the article, "Of the two million soldiers the United States sent to France in World War I, he is the only one left." Buckles told the author in an interview: "For a long time I've felt that there should be more recognition of the surviving veterans of World War I." The author added: "Now that group is, more or less, him." [1]

Richard Rubin, author of the op-ed article, has written a book, *The Last of the Doughboys*, in which he told the story of his interviews with

---

1. *New York Times* (Nov. 12, 2007) A21

several dozen veterans of the First World War. For the project he was unable to secure a list of the remaining veterans from any sources in the United States. Neither the Department of Veteran Affairs nor any of the veterans' organizations could supply him with any names. The only place where he could find such a list was from the government of France!

November 11th was proclaimed Armistice Day in 1919 to remember the signing the previous year of the agreement that brought an end to the First World War, the war that was supposed to make the world safe for democracy and end all wars but did not succeed. The war started again in 1939 in what we call the Second World War, but was just a continuation of the First. On June 1, 1954, President Dwight D. Eisenhower signed an act passed by the U.S. Congress, "to honor veterans on the eleventh day of November of each year . . . a day dedicated to world peace." Unfortunately, for a number of years, Veterans Day was observed on the second Monday of November, regardless of the date, until it was finally moved back to November 11th.

This only begins to answer the question posed to Mallard about the difference between Memorial Day and Veterans Day. First, we can honor the veterans and provide resources for their return to civilian life, not just annual ceremonies. Second, we can remember Armistice Day as the end of the First World War, as declared by President Woodrow Wilson. Third, in keeping with the 1954 declaration of Veterans Day, we can dedicate ourselves to world peace.

In the interest of full disclosure, I am not a veteran, but in my long career as a clergyman I have visited veterans in their homes and hospitals and have participated in ceremonies, concerts, religious services, and other events for the purpose of honoring veterans. Family members, on both my mother's and dad's side, have served in most of the wars of this country. For example, my father's immigrant ancestor fought in the bloody battle of Lake George, NY, in the French and Indian War, and one of his sons was in the Revolutionary War militia in what became the State of Vermont. On my mother's side one ancestor was a Fife Major at Valley Forge. My maternal grandfather was in the Twenty-Seventh Regiment, Connecticut Volunteers, and fought in the horrendous battle of Fredericksburg. My mother's youngest brother was a naval Ensign in the First World War. My older brother was in the First Marine Division in the Second World War, was wounded in the invasion of Peleliu, fought at Okinawa, and assisted in the occupation of China after the war. My younger brother was in Korea, and one of my cousins was killed in Vietnam. We found his name on the Vietnam Veterans Memorial in Washington, DC.

In time for our country's Bicentennial in 1976 the movie *Nashville* came out, and it began with the song, "200 Years," sung by Henry Gibson. In the opening lines he mentioned an ancestor who fought in the Revolutionary War at Bunker Hill, his father in France in the First World War, and his brother who fought with General George Patton in the Second World War.

We are indebted to our veterans over many generations who have not only kept this nation free but have gone overseas time and time again to stop invasions, liberate countries, and defeat dictatorships and totalitarian regimes which have threatened to take over the world or to conquer an entire region of it. These veterans have sacrificed years of their lives, leaving school or work, family and community in order to serve their country in time of need. Movies, like Ken Burns's documentary, *The War*, numerous books, articles, films, and TV programs have dramatized the horror and insanity of war, and have shown why veterans returning home have been unable to talk about their experiences. However, these productions, as well as war memorials, like the ones in Washington, DC, for Vietnam and World War II, have helped some veterans to share their stories.

At the end of the twentieth century and the beginning of the twenty-first there has emerged a growing body of literature on the veterans of the Second World War and their readjustment to civilian life. Acquaintance with this literature will change forever how we view veterans and Veterans Day.

The Greatest Generation

Inspired by the veterans who returned to the Normandy beaches for the fortieth and fiftieth anniversaries of D-Day, Tom Brokaw of NBC News wrote the book, *The Greatest Generation*, and it was published in 1998. In it he told the stories of about fifty people and members of two groups who had grown up in the Great Depression, served the country in many ways in the Second World War, and then contributed to the post-war economy and prosperity. In response to a question from Tim Russert on *Meet the Press,* Brokaw said that this was "the greatest generation any society has ever produced." Not only had they survived privation and scarcity in the 1930s, but they had sacrificed years of their lives to fight in two parts of the world, Europe and the Pacific, in the 1940s, and then returned to families and communities, schools and jobs. Brokaw called them "ordinary people," who served in the Army, Navy, Air Corps, Marines, Coast Guard and Merchant Marine, and then built careers in insurance, real estate, printing, highways, schools, and many other enterprises.

One veteran represented a group which called themselves ROMEO, "Retired Old Men Eating Out." Included in the book was what Brokaw called "heroes," men who received the Medal of Honor and other awards. There was a section devoted to women who served in the armed forces as WACS, WAVES, Nurse Corps, and in other ways. Some had to struggle with prejudice and discrimination because they were African-American, Hispanic, or Asian. The author devoted a section to the love stories and successful marriages which grew out of the war period. There was also a part about "Famous People," such as President George H. W. Bush, who was in the Navy Air Corps, journalist Ben Bradlee, writer Art Buchwald, pundit Andy Rooney, Chef Julia Child, and others. The final section was about people who became U.S. Senators, Cabinet officers, presidential advisors, and historians. Some of the people profiled were not veterans but worked on the "home front," especially some women who made important contributions because the men had been called away.

A central theme of the book was gratitude, deep appreciation to the members of this generation who had sacrificed so much and contributed substantially to make the country what it was. Another theme was the sense of values maintained by these people; according to Brokaw, they "stayed true to their values of personal responsibility, duty, honor, and faith."

Brokaw's book struck a chord and provided a lasting label for an entire generation of cohorts, who were in turn the mothers and fathers of the "baby boomers." The term became a part of our lexicon and consciousness, and has influenced other books, speeches, museums, and memorials. In my hometown the mini-bus for the Senior Center was emblazoned with the words, "The Greatest Generation."

Brokaw was overwhelmed by letters and messages from so many people that it led to two other books, *The Greatest Generation Speaks: Letters and Reflections* in 1999 and *An Album of Memories: Personal Histories from the Greatest Generation* in 2001. There were those who felt that the book helped them to understand what the generation went through and enabled veterans to share memories that had been previously hidden. Some people were not happy with any category of veterans overlooked in the first book. There were letters from those who did the "grunt" work, from chaplains, from spouses, from children and grandchildren, and some letters had been written from the war front itself. What they revealed was the strength of the bonds that had been formed, the deep affection and appreciation for those who had served, and the importance of the reunions of military units.

The last book in the trilogy was like a scrapbook or album of the Second World War, with photos, maps, telegrams, newspaper articles, war souvenirs, posters, copies of hand-written letters, and much more from both the front lines and the home front. Beginning with the days of the Great Depression and the bombing of Pearl Harbor, the volume covered the war in Europe, in the Pacific, the situation at home, and ended with some reflections. Each section began with an introduction by Brokaw, and there was a detailed chronology of the events in the two theaters of war.

There were those who were critical of the notion of "The Greatest Generation." The historian Arthur Schlesinger, Jr. wrote in an article in the *AARP Bulletin* on "The Rediscovery of World War II" that the greatest generation consisted of those who fought the Revolutionary War and designed the U.S. Constitution. Another historian Joseph J. Ellis concurred in his book, *Founding Brothers: The Revolutionary Generation.* One author, Charles P. Pierce, wrote in *Esquire* about "The Complaint: The Beatification of the Greatest Generation."

In 2008 there was published the most comprehensive critique entitled *Myth and the Greatest Generation: A Social History of Americans in World War II* by Kenneth D. Rose. The author recognized that veterans are dying at the rate of 1,100 a day, that the war is receding from memory, and that there is a tendency to romanticize, sanitize, or even to re-write the history. There were at least three major corrections: the horror, savagery, and trauma of the war experiences had been glossed over; the home front was not idyllic, but produced broken marriages, juvenile delinquency, racial and labor unrest, and a thriving black market; the generation was not as patriotic or religious as it has been portrayed. Rose believed that a nostalgic myth had been created, and rather than beatifying or canonizing the veterans it would be better to humanize them.

Readjustment to Civilian Life

After the liberation of Paris by the Allied forces, famed war correspondent Ernie Pyle sat down under an apple tree in an orchard outside the city and wrote the last chapter of his book, *Brave Men*, in which he addressed the American people in the following way:

"Thousands of our men will be returning to you after Europe. They have been gone a long time and they have seen and done and felt things you cannot know. They will be changed. They will have to learn how to adjust themselves to peace."[2]

Pyle himself never made it back to the States. After the war was won in Europe, he was transferred to the Pacific and was killed in Okinawa on April 18, 1945.

Mark D. Van Ells wrote his 1999 doctoral dissertation at the University of Wisconsin, Madison, on the subject of the readjustment of Second World War veterans to civilian life, and it was published in 2001 with the title, *To Hear Only Thunder Again: America's World War II Veterans Come Home*. The title was based on another part of Ernie Pyle's last chapter, where he described a severe thunderstorm in the French countryside, and it was half over before Pyle and his companions realized it was just thunder and not artillery. In his comments on the Van Ells book, Thomas Childers of the University of Pennsylvania recognized it as an important contribution to the vast literature on the Second World War. The library shelves are filled with books on the war, including histories of individual soldiers, battles, military units, campaigns, theaters of war, but there was not much about the veterans after they returned home. Van Ells recognized this and sought to rectify it.

With a special emphasis on the situation in Wisconsin, Van Ells looked at the various problems in civilian life and the variety of services provided by local, state, and federal agencies with the support of the public. He examined the social and cultural adjustments, the medical issues, physical and psychological, the educational situation, and the problems of employment and housing. Among the emotional problems identified were disillusionment, bitterness, resentment, hatred of the German and Japanese enemies, and restlessness. He concluded that readjustment after the Second World War went more smoothly than after other wars because of the multitude of services and benefits which were provided. The programs were flexible and carried out on an individual basis—no one program fit all—but they worked. It was clear that some veterans did not gain as much, because of disability, prejudice, racial and even gender discrimination. Van Ells felt that veterans from Korea and Vietnam did not have the same public support and the programs were not as effective.

2. Pyle, *Brave Men*, 320

While Van Ells discussed the problems of returning veterans in a general, almost encyclopedic way, other authors have personalized the struggle in their own narratives. Julia Collins wrote *My Father's War: A Memoir* about a member of the Fifth Marine Division, who survived the battle of Okinawa. According to the daughter, her father's life came to a "standstill" in 1946, as he brought the war home with him. He suffered nightmares and "survivor's guilt," and lost himself in drinking and other "diversions," like infidelity. The author pointed out that many veterans were scarred physically and emotionally by the war and remained close-mouthed about what they went through. Collins was in contact with another Marine survivor of Okinawa, William Manchester, historian-in-residence at Wesleyan University for many years. Manchester had written a number of acclaimed books, but was unable to deal with his war experience until he returned to Okinawa in 1978. The result the following year was the book, *Goodbye, Darkness: A Memoir of the Pacific War.*

Several years after Julia Collins's book was published, Tom Mathews wrote *Our Fathers' War: Growing Up in the Shadow of the Greatest Generation*, in which he followed the careers of ten veterans, beginning with his father, who had been with the Tenth Mountain Division fighting in Italy. Mathews grew up in Utah, but the other veterans were in the Long Island area and included a Jewish airman who was in a Nazi POW camp, several infantrymen, two of whom were in the "Battle of the Bulge," one in Army intelligence and another in supply, and a member of the "Tuskegee Airmen." Some of them were wounded, suffered combat fatigue or what was later diagnosed as Post Traumatic Stress Disorder. The Tuskegee Airman encountered segregation even in North Africa and remembered German POWs being allowed in camp posts when African-Americans were excluded. The author felt alienated from his father because of not doing a "manly thing" as a boy, but found reconciliation, when the two of them went to Italy and traced the campaign of the Tenth Mountain Division.

Kevin Coyne wrote the story of six veterans from his hometown of Freehold, New Jersey, in the book, *Marching Home: To War and Back with the Men of One American Town.* Half of the book was focused on their experiences in the war, whether on a ship in the Mediterranean and the Pacific, in the jungles of New Guinea, in a bombardment group in England, in a segregated "colored" unit of engineers in Europe, and as a waist gunner on a B-26 Marauder out of England. They returned to Freehold after the war and found a variety of jobs. They lived through the closing of the largest industry in town, a fire that burned part of the business district, a 1969 confrontation between Blacks and Whites and a near riot and shooting. Several of their sons served in the Vietnam War. These veterans saw vast changes in their community, including suburban sprawl.

The last chapter was a moving account of the fiftieth anniversary of the end of the war, in which four of the six participated. Several had lost their wives and remarried. One traveled back to Australia with his "war bride" for one last visit with her parents. Another met the family of a wounded soldier he had rescued from the front line of a battle. What they all shared in common was an awareness of the changes in the country over fifty years, from a concern for the "common good" and the good of the community, to a struggle for personal rights and privileges. One veteran observed that the country was "not so much a settled nation as a sustained act of will."

Thomas Childers, who had commented on the Van Ells book, made his own contribution to the growing literature on the subject with his book, *Soldier From the War Returning: The Greatest Generation's Troubled Homecoming from World War II*. Having told the story of two military units and their war stories in previous books, he turned his attention to three individual veterans, including his own father, who was in the 390th Bomb Group. A second veteran was an airman in a B-17, who bailed out when his plane was hit and suffered in a POW camp. The third was an infantryman in the invasion of Italy, who was hit by a bomb in German territory and lost both his legs. Childers's father, on returning home, dealt with unemployment, lack of housing, the skyrocketing cost of living, and estrangement from his wife. He was disillusioned and bitter, left his family for a period of time, but was never divorced. The airman became a medical doctor, but his nightmares from the war continued and he suffered outbursts of anger and temper. Divorced and remarried, he was diagnosed with PTSD and became aware that the war had never ended for him. The infantryman, with his disability, faced the greatest hurdles. He became alienated from his wife and children, divorced and remarried, but even his second marriage didn't work out. The Childers book was set within the context of the many articles about returning servicemen which were published at the time of the war and also within the framework of the research that has been done regarding the physical and emotional legacy of the war.

"The Best Years of Our Lives"

The award-winning film *The Best Years of Our Lives* was a classic portrayal of the struggle of three veterans to re-adjust to civilian life after the Second World War. Directed by William Wyler, it won seven Academy Awards in 1947, including best picture, best director, best actor (Fredric March), best screenplay (Robert E. Sherwood), best supporting actor (Harold Russell), best film editing and best musical score. In addition, Russell won an honorary Oscar "for bringing hope and courage to his fellow veterans"; he was the only one in film history to win two Oscars for the same role in a film. The movie told the story of a sergeant who had led a platoon in the Pacific, an Army Air Corps Captain on a B-17 in bombing runs over Europe, and a sailor who lost both hands in an explosion on his ship in the Pacific. The three met on a plane trip back to their hometown, and their lives became entwined as they tried to establish themselves in the post-war period.

Along the way the film captured many of the problems faced by veterans as they returned home. The sergeant, with a grown daughter and college-age son, returned to his family and received a good job at the local bank as a loan officer, but was rebuked by his manager when he gave a loan to another veteran without collateral. The sergeant became a heavy drinker and, in a somewhat inebriated state, spoke at a banquet and after a shaky start concluded with the thought that in gambling with depositors' money they were "gambling on the future of the country."

Reunited with his attractive wife, the Captain had trouble finding a job and exhausted their savings. He discovered that his wife was disappointed that he was no longer the dashing young officer in uniform that she had remembered, and she was having an affair and wanted a divorce. He ended up back at the drugstore where he used to work, but he was fired when he hit a customer who claimed that we had fought the wrong enemy. Leaving home, the Captain visited a scrap yard for old planes and climbed into the nose of a B-17, where he had flashbacks of bombing missions, from which he had suffered recurring nightmares. He was roused by a worker and offered a job helping to convert the metal into homes for veterans.

With the loss of both hands, the sailor faced the greatest challenge, but he had learned the use of prosthetic hooks. He was engaged to a young woman, but her family questioned whether he had a future. He showed anger when treated like a freak and curiosity by neighborhood children, but maintained his confidence and rejected any kind of pity. His fiancé loved him despite the handicap and they were married at the end of the film. The Captain, meanwhile, began a relationship with the sergeant's daughter.

The film was considered so important that Kenneth D. Rose discussed it in his book, *Myth and the Greatest Generation*. Rose pointed out that Harold Russell was chosen for the film by Wyler despite the fact that he was not a professional actor. Russell had served in the Army and lost his hands in a dynamite explosion. The director had seen Russell in an Army Signal Corps documentary, *Diary of a Sergeant*. According to Rose, the film did not moralize and did not suggest an easy or happy ending for the veterans. In a sense, they paid the cost of the war even when the war was long over.

To Honor Veterans

Honoring veterans means much more than medals and monuments, parades and pageantry. First, it means understanding who they are and what they went through. Second, it means providing the resources so that they can get on with their lives after the war.

Veterans do not want to be thanked. They feel strongly that they did a job, that they responded to the call of their country, that they saw it as their duty. They also don't like to be called "heroes." Indeed, there are heroes among them, especially those who have risked their lives to save others. However, wearing the uniform doesn't automatically make one a hero.

Most fundamental to the understanding of veterans is the realization that one can never appreciate what they have experienced, unless one was in the jungle, the foxhole, the plane or the ship alongside them. Those on the front lines of battle witnessed carnage, brutality, savagery, horrors that cannot be described. This is why it is almost impossible for them to talk about it. Whether on the front lines or in supporting roles, they lost buddies and best friends and often suffer "survivor's guilt," wondering why was he killed and not me? Was it just luck or was there no bullet with my name on it? Those in combat experienced a camaraderie that is impossible to duplicate in civilian life. They were bound together, looking out for each other, a "band of brothers," fighting for a common cause, a transcendent purpose, a single-minded mission, that eludes the comprehension of non-combatants.

Much has been written about the "common good," the dedication to the welfare of the community, the need for cooperation, which characterizes the military. In the real world the common good is replaced by the pursuit of selfish gain, assertion of individual rights and privileges, dog-eat-dog competition to get ahead of the other person. There is a sense of "I've got mine, the hell with everybody else." Columnist David Brooks has commented on the "atomization of society," which fosters a libertarian distrust of authority and institutions, the spread of cynicism and the fraying of the social fabric. Other commentators have pointed out that the new technologies tend to separate and isolate people rather than bring them together. Veterans, who have been trained and disciplined to work for the greater good, can experience a sense of disillusionment.

Veterans need the resources to enable them to get re-established in civilian life at their own pace and in accordance with their own needs. Their lives have been disrupted, and they have been removed from their homes and communities, schools and work. Concerted efforts are needed to help them make up for lost time with a kind of "affirmative action" or re-compensation. This is especially true for those who have been disabled in some way, those who have been maimed, left with loss of limb, sight or hearing. Medical facilities need to be expanded to care for veterans. In addition, there are those who have suffered psychological and emotional damage, what has been diagnosed in 1980 as PTSD, which was the "combat fatigue" of the Second World War, the "shell shock" of the First World War, and even the "soldier's heart" of the Civil War. It has been defined as the effect of extreme stress on the psyche resulting in depression, anxiety, flashbacks, recurrent nightmares, and avoidance of reminders of the war.

Honoring veterans means giving them the best kind of health care, educational opportunity, vocational assistance, decent housing, and a place in our communities that goes beyond special days and veterans' clubs.

It was shocking to learn in the first decade of the twenty-first century that one-fourth of the homeless people in our country are veterans, that their suicide rate is climbing, and that there is a backlog in the processing of veterans' pensions and benefits. Every war has produced thousands of veterans who are not only maimed physically, but also mentally and emotionally, scarred not only in body, but also in spirit and soul. The test of a great nation is how it treats the people it sends into "harm's way," whether it forgets them or provides the counseling, support, resources and services that will enable them to resume their places in our communities and in their families with pride and dignity.

Veterans appreciate their benefits, but they want to continue to serve their country, even though they may no longer be in the military. They want to educate the general public, especially the young, about their wartime experiences, and they want to promote patriotism through the proper use of the flag and the honoring of memorials and Veterans Day.

To Remember the Armistice

What is distinctive about Veterans Day is that it began as the anniversary of the end of a war, the cessation of hostilities in the First World War at 11 a.m. on the 11th day of the 11th month, November 1918. The armistice agreement had been signed at 5 a.m., but hundreds of soldiers were killed before the truce officially went into effect. Any observance of Veterans Day has to take into account that war and the American soldiers who fought in it. Happily, that process has been made much easier by the publication of Richard Rubin's book, *The Last of the Doughboys: The Forgotten Generation and Their Forgotten War*. The title alone bespeaks the common lack of knowledge and attention to those who preceded the "Greatest Generation." Incidentally, Rubin has stated that it is a "dicey proposition" to pin that label on a generation.

In 2003 the author embarked on a project to interview the last remaining veterans of that war. The Dept. of Veterans Affairs had estimated earlier that there might be 1,500 veterans still living, but that number was reduced to less than 200. Neither the VA nor the American Legion or the VFW could supply their names. However, the French president Jacques Chirac planned in 1998 to give their highest military award, the Legion of Honor, to Americans who fought in France and were still alive. The French government tracked down hundreds of veterans and presented them with a medal and a certificate in ceremonies all over the United States. With the help of the French embassy, Rubin compiled a list of names and their hometowns and was able to visit and interview several dozen who were between 101 and 113 years old.

What resulted was not a history of the war but a veritable social history of the country at the time of the war and what happened to the veterans who fought in it. The book is based not only on multiple interviews, but also on many books written about units and campaigns and memoirs by soldiers, including the popular *Over the Top* and the novel *Company K*. Rubin had also collected an immense amount of material, the many songs written during the war at the peak of popularity of "tin pan alley." These songs had an almost journalistic ability to convey the moods and attitudes of the American people. Prior to the United States entering the war on April 6, 1917, the mood was isolationist, exemplified by the re-election of

President Woodrow Wilson with the slogan, "He kept us out of the war." After war was declared, nothing could be said against it, and hundreds went to prison because of the Espionage Act of 1917, amended in 1918.

About two million soldiers served in the American Expeditionary Forces under General John Pershing. Another two million were in uniform ready to cross the ocean. Over 117,000 were killed, and hundreds of thousands were wounded. Most of their fighting was in France alongside French, British, and other troops, and they experienced the trench warfare and "no man's land" which characterized the war for nearly three years. They were subject to constant artillery fire, bombs from the new airplanes, mustard gas, grenades, rifle and machine gun fire. The Americans tipped the balance in favor of the Allies, fighting in such places as Seicheprey, the Somme, Chateau-Thierry, Belleau Wood, the Second Marne, Saint-Mihiel, and the final Meuse-Argonne offensive. Rubin also interviewed a veteran who had been sent to Siberia, Russia, to protect a shipment of American arms, and also an American citizen who had fought with the Canadian army. There were also those in the United States Navy who never made it to French soil and were not on France's list, and two women who enlisted in the Navy but never went overseas.

Pertinent to an understanding of veterans and Veterans Day was Rubin's discussion of the difficulties faced by the veterans after the war. Many had lost their livelihoods and couldn't find jobs. Farms, businesses, even homes were lost, and the Great Depression exacerbated the situation. The U.S. Congress had established the Veterans Bureau in 1921 in order to help the many wounded veterans and to administer insurance claims. According to Rubin, many veterans got no payments at all because funds were embezzled. Hospitals and other facilities were not built, medical supplies were missing, and many claims were denied. A bill was passed to provide compensation, vetoed by President Calvin Coolidge, and then the veto was over-ridden by Congress, but payments were postponed until 1945.

This led to the "bonus army" march on Washington, DC, in 1932 to lobby for a new bill that would pay bonuses right away. Despite an encampment by 20,000 veterans and their families, the bill was defeated in the Senate after it had passed the House. General Douglas MacArthur was ordered to evict the bonus marchers from their encampments around the Capitol, and he used bayonets, tanks, and even gas to drive them out. Many veterans were injured, many were arrested, and the infant member of one veteran's family died of poison gas. This incident involving veterans on American soil may have helped propel the Congress to create a stronger program of services and benefits after the Second World War.

The Armistice of November 11, 1918, brought an end to the First World War to the great joy of millions of soldiers as well as civilians, but the harsh, punitive terms laid the basis for a resumption of the war in 1939.

Dedicated to World Peace

The purpose of Veterans Day is not only to honor veterans but also is dedicated to world peace. Ernie Pyle wrote to the American people in the conclusion of *Brave Men* that the soldiers need to be adjusted to peace. One veteran of the invasion of Omaha Beach at Normandy described the terrible experience of climbing over dead bodies on the beach, and said: "What a waste!" A friend of mine and a Boy Scout co-leader was killed in the early days of the Korean War. At the fiftieth anniversary of his death a reception was held for some friends and family, and one of his brothers said of such a talented leader: "What a waste!" At the anniversaries of the landings at Normandy both Presidents Reagan and Clinton and commentators Walter Cronkite and Andy Rooney spoke of the need for peace. One of the best ways of honoring our veterans and remembering the Armistice is to make war obsolete as a instrument of national policy. The world is too small and the weapons of mass destruction too available for wiping life off this planet. Yet, with constant wars, it has become the "new normal." Instead of a course of last resort, it has been used early and even in a preemptive way.

In 1969, after hearing the news from Vietnam about the massacre at the village of Song My or My Lai, I wrote a letter to the President of the United States, with a copy to *LIFE* magazine, which was never published. In part of the letter I said:

> "When will we learn that war is not the way to win peace, and that no one wins a war anymore? Why do we continue to glorify the wars in our history and reserve our highest awards and most numerous monuments for warriors, wars and battlefields? Why is "duty to country" and "supreme sacrifice" designated only for those who fight and are killed in battle? When are we as a nation going to put our full weight behind an international peace-keeping force under the United Nations and stop our unilateral efforts to police the entire world?"[3]

3. Kathan. Unpublished letter to *LIFE*, (Dec. 25, 1969)

The late John Lennon sang: "Give peace a chance." The Highwaymen sang in "The Universal Soldier" about the soldiers from every nation who think they can put an end to war, and know that they never will. The Book of Ecclesiastes in the Hebrew Scriptures stated: "For everything there is a season and a time for every matter under heaven; a time for war and a time for peace." The Hebrew Scriptures also include the vision of Isaiah: "they shall beat their swords into plowshares, and their spears into pruning hooks; nation shall not lift up sword against nation, neither shall they learn war anymore."[4] In the Christian Scriptures Jesus is quoted in the Sermon on the Mount in one of the Beatitudes: "Blessed are the peacemakers, for they will be called children of God."[5]

Some years ago a Sr. High youth group in a church wanted to lead a worship service on the theme of peace and wanted to use the song, "Let there be peace on earth," but were afraid there might be a copyright problem. Jill Jackson, who had written and composed the song with her husband Sy Miller, was contacted in California, and she said that they had prepared the song for just such an occasion, and the group had her permission. The entire congregation sang it as part of the service.

The song was a favorite of a friend of mine, Roy Schellhardt, who served in the U.S. Marine Corps in the Second World War. He loved to sing: we sang together in the Senior Choir of the Prospect Congregational Church, he sang in a group in the Prospect Senior Center called the "Songbirds," and he led a sing-a-long every month at the Glendale Nursing Center in Naugatuck, Connecticut, where he had lived for over six years. The climax of the sing-a-long was the singing of his favorite song, "Let there be peace on earth, and let it begin with me."

Veterans like Roy, even more than other people, can take the leadership to find and develop the ways that lead to peace, because of all that they have been through. On Veterans Day, we can honor our veterans, remember the Armistice, and work with veterans to dedicate that day and every day to the pursuit of peace.

4. Isa 2:4b (New Revised Standard Version)
5. Matt 5:9 (NRSV)

CHAPTER 10

Thanksgiving, Prayer, and Praise

THANKSGIVING DAY

THANKSGIVING IS A QUINTESSENTIAL American holiday, steeped in tradition, packed with sentiment, and dripping in nostalgia. It evokes the Norman Rockwell painting of grandmother placing the roasted turkey on the family dinner table and a Currier and Ives print, "Home for Thanksgiving"; it recites the verses of "Over the river and through the woods"; it echoes the translation of a Dutch hymn, "We gather together to ask the Lord's blessing"; and it repeats the time-honored question of parents to their children, "What are you thankful for?" Its origin is enveloped in the very beginnings of our country and the story of the first settlers of Plymouth, Massachusetts, who later would be called the Pilgrim fathers and mothers. Their perilous trip over the ocean in the *Mayflower* is a familiar one, along with their first brutal year when half of them died, their befriending and assistance by local Wampanoags and the three-day feast held at the end of 1621. There were earlier acts or rituals of thanksgiving in the new world, in Texas, Florida, Virginia, even in what is now Maine, but the event in Plymouth has captured the imagination of the American people and has established a custom that has continued to the present day. The town of Plymouth calls itself "America's home town," and not without justification.

TIME magazine published an essay in 1989 by Walter Shapiro entitled "Why We've Failed to Ruin Thanksgiving." He wrote: "More than any other date on the calendar, Thanksgiving has remained private and personal, devoid of the tinsel trappings that mar the rest of contemporary life." He continued: "No other holiday brings generations together without the lure of anything more tangible than a good dinner."

Since the end of the nineteenth century there have been football games and other sporting events and since 1924 the Macy's Christmas parade, but there are no Thanksgiving presents or shopping season, and Thanksgiving cards exist but few are mailed. Schools and businesses and stores are closed. Despite the more recent effort to open stores late on Thursday to begin the "black Friday" Christmas shopping day, Shapiro's words still ring true: "In a nation where the mall never palls and seven-days-a-week shopping seems enshrined as a civil religion, Thanksgiving stands out as an oasis of tranquility and a reminder of the values that once tempered America's materialism."[1]

Thanksgiving is celebrated more than any other national holiday; most Americans observe a ritual of sitting down and eating a meal, whether it is the traditional turkey and all the trimmings, or other foods of ethnic origin. Despite the fact that it was originated by a small Congregational church group whom we know as the Pilgrims, it is a day shared by people of all races, religions, and national backgrounds; even the most recent immigrant is caught up in the festivities that remember those early newcomers to these shores, who ate a pot-luck meal with a group of Native Americans.

Thanksgiving is also unique in that it is the only national holiday that began as a local or regional one and became national. It was primarily be-cause of the lobbying by Sarah Josepha Hale, who finally succeeded when Abraham Lincoln issued a Proclamation for a National Thanksgiving Day in 1863 in the midst of the horrific Civil War, setting the last Thursday of November. The emotional attachment to that day was demonstrated in 1939 during the Great Depression when people were outraged because Franklin Delano Roosevelt wanted to change Thanksgiving to the fourth Thursday in order to begin the Christmas shopping season earlier. Finally, in 1941 the U.S. Congress established the fourth Thursday of November as the annual Thanksgiving Day, and it has never been changed to a Monday!

On a personal note, Thanksgiving was a very important holiday in our family. Among my mother's prized possessions were a framed print of "The First Thanksgiving—as imagined by Jennie Brownscombe" (1914), a miniature replica of the *Mayflower*, and a large John Rogers's plaster sculpture of John Alden and Priscilla Mullins ("Why don't you speak for yourself, John") from 1885. In 1945 my grandmother offered prayer at the

1. Shapiro, *TIME*, (Nov. 23, 1989), 94

Thanksgiving table, thanking God for the end of the war and the survival of my older brother and his returning home from years in the Pacific with the First Marine Division. That was my grandmother's last Thanksgiving, since she died the following year. My mother insisted that we go to the annual Thanksgiving church service in spite of the fact that my high school football team was playing that morning, and I was sports editor of the high school paper.

In 1952, when my wife and I lived in the Netherlands, the American Embassy planned a Thanksgiving service for all the Fulbright students and others at the old Peter's Church in Leiden, followed by a turkey dinner in a nearby restaurant. Over the years our family entertained many students from overseas on the holiday; one year it was the son of the president of Doshisha University in Japan. In 1963 I wrote and produced a Thanksgiving pageant at the large Mayflower Congregational Church in Minneapolis, and it was repeated in 1988 in Cheshire, Connecticut. The following year I preached at an inter-faith service on Thanksgiving eve on the subject, "More than a harvest festival."

Books About Thanksgiving

There are lots of books about Thanksgiving Day in libraries, but they are mostly for children. There are at least six books for adults written since 1949, an older book from 1895, two contemporary accounts of the Pilgrims, two books of Pilgrim history, *Saints and Strangers*, by George F. Willison, and *Mayflower: A Story of Courage, Community and War*, by Nathaniel Philbrick, which gave little attention to the 1621 feast, and two resources from the Plimouth Plantation, *The Thanksgiving Primer* and *1621: A New Look at Thanksgiving*.

Bradford's History and Mourt's Relation

One book is *Of Plymouth Plantation, 1620–1647*, by William Bradford, who took the place of John Carver as Governor of the colony. The other is *A Relation or Journall of the beginnings and proceedings of the English Plantation setled at Plimouth in New England by certain English Adventurers both Merchants and others*, commonly known as *Mourt's Relation*. Bradford's manuscript had been copied into the Plymouth Church records and was used by other historians, but was not published in its entirety until 1856, but Alexander Young's *Chronicles of the Pilgrim Fathers* in 1841 printed parts and included a footnote reporting that the 1621 event was the "First Thanksgiving." A recent edition of Bradford's history was edited by Samuel Eliot Morison, professor at Harvard, and was published in 1954. *Mourt's Relation* was published in England in 1622 and included excerpts from the journals of Bradford and Edward Winslow.

Bradford's history did not describe a feast in 1621, but reported: "All the summer there was no want . . . " and "Which made many afterwards write so largely of their plenty here to their friends in England, which were not feigned but true reports." Included in *Mourt's Relation* was the letter of Winslow to a friend in England, and this was considered the first description of that Thanksgiving feast:

> "Our harvest being gotten in, our Governor sent four men on fowling, that we might after a more special manner rejoice together, after we had gathered the fruit of our labours. They four in one day killed as much fowl as, with a little help beside, served the Company almost a week. At which time, amongst other recreations, we exercised our arms, many of the Indians coming amongst us, and amongst the rest their greatest king, Massasoit with some 90 men, whom for three days we entertained and feasted. And they went out and killed five deer which they brought to the plantation and bestowed on our Governor and upon the Captain and others."[2]

No date was given for the three-day festival.

Love's Fast and Thanksgiving Days

In 1895 the results of an exhaustive study by a Congregational minister, William DeLoss Love, were published in a book, *The Fast and Thanksgiving Days of New England*. The author surveyed the history of days of "Publick Humiliation" or Fasts and days of Thanksgiving, which were an important part of the Anglican and Puritan traditions in England. These were not annual events, but occasional days of fasting and prayer because of dire emergencies, such as prolonged drought, or days of feasting and prayer because of special acts of God's providence and grace. Sometimes the fast would lead right into a feast.

Love described the ritual of a Puritan day of thanksgiving and said regarding the 1621 three-day festival in Plymouth: "It was not a Thanksgiving

2. Heath, *A Journal of the Pilgrims at Plymouth*, 60–61

at all, judged by their Puritan customs, which they kept in 1621, but as we look back upon it after nearly three centuries, it seems so wonderfully like the day we love that we claim it as the progenitor of our harvest feasts."[3]

The Lintons' We Gather Together

In their 1949 book, *We Gather Together: The Story of Thanksgiving*, Ralph and Adelin Linton have explained the ancient tradition of harvest festivals, going back to the Israelites, as recorded in the Hebrew Bible, the Greeks, Romans and other civilizations. The Yale anthropologist and his wife focused on the "Harvest Home" celebrations in England, a custom brought across the ocean to the new world by the Pilgrims, and also on the important role of Tisquantum or Squanto, whom they considered a "neglected hero." It was also pointed out that Native Americans on the eastern seaboard observed a kind of harvest festival with a ritual called the Green Corn Dance. The Lintons have suggested that Massasoit and the ninety men came to the Pilgrims' 1621 feast, believing that it was a harvest festival. However, the authors conceded that July 30, 1623, may have been the first real day of Thanksgiving, since the Governor proclaimed it for "both religious and social celebration."

Appelbaum's An American Holiday

"The Shaping of the American Thanksgiving" could be another name for the 1984 book, *Thanksgiving: An American Holiday, An American History*, by Diana Karter Appelbaum, a researcher and author of historical pieces. More than any other person, she has chronicled the history, development, and expansion of this holiday from a regional observance to a truly national one. It was unclear to her that the 1621 feast could be called the "First Thanksgiving." She recognized that it did not spring "full grown and completely armed with roast turkey and cranberry sauce from the head of a Pilgrim Father," but evolved and changed with the history of the country. Along the way she has described days of Thanksgiving proclaimed by the Continental Congress, the migration of New Englanders to the West, the many proclamations by governors and a few by U.S. Presidents until 1863,

3. Love, *Fast and Thanksgiving Days of New England*, 69

and the attempts to provide a Thanksgiving dinner for soldiers in the various wars and for Americans wherever they may be located in the world.

Hodgson's Great and Godly Adventure

A British journalist, Godfrey Hodgson, wrote a book in 2006, *A Great and Godly Adventure: The Pilgrims and the Myth of the First Thanksgiving.* As the author also of *The Myth of American Exceptionalism,* he has sought to debunk the myths that have gathered around these early settlers of Plymouth. For one, they were not called Pilgrims until William Bradford wrote his history. Referring to their departure from the Netherlands, Bradford wrote: "So they left that goodly and pleasant city which had been their resting place near twelve years, but they knew they were pilgrims, and looked not much on those things, but lift up their eyes to the heavens, their dearest country, and quieted their spirits."[4]

For another, Plymouth Rock was not their landing place. It was not mentioned by any eyewitnesses. The legend was born in 1741, and the rock split when it was moved in 1774. When a wharf was going to replace it in the nineteenth century, it was iconized and a canopy or temple built over it, in part to keep souvenir hunters from chipping away at it.

Hodgson also reminded his readers that the *Mayflower Compact* was not the foundation of a new nation or government, but was a covenant or agreement to establish a congregation in the new world and was signed on board the *Mayflower* in order to bind the diverse group of people together. (What Hodgson forgot was that the congregation had been created many years earlier in Scrooby, England; and that what the Compact created was a "body politic.") Appelbaum called it the "first such voluntary constitution in the colonies."

As far as the first Thanksgiving is concerned, Hodgson felt that a relatively insignificant encounter between the Pilgrims and the Indians has been elevated to a "dominant event in the national narrative." He called it one of the "pious fictions of the American political religion." However, he recognized that the myth was a "powerful and virtuous symbol." It was better to thank God for prosperity and freedom than defeat over enemies.

4. Bradford, *History of Plymouth Plantation*, 47

Colman's True Story of Thanksgiving

Although intended for a younger audience, the 2008 book by Penny Colman, *Thanksgiving: The True Story*, was a concise and accurate assessment of the competing claims for the "First Thanksgiving," (she has listed twelve) and an analysis of how the 1621 feast won out. As a member of the faculty of Queens College, City University of New York, she has done considerable research in the primary documents and has carried out an extensive survey of what people believe about Thanksgiving and how they celebrate it. Most important, she has not regarded the 1621 story of "Pilgrims and Indians" as myth or fiction, but as an attempt by Americans to tell the story of the founding of the country. According to Colman, every country has a story about how and when it began. For Americans it was a story that communicated particular values and united an increasingly diverse population around specific beliefs. A hymn in 1838 by Leonard Bacon had the words, "Laws, freedom, truth, and faith in God Came with those exiles o'er the waves."

Baker's Biography of Thanksgiving

A more recent book was *Thanksgiving: The Biography of an American Holiday* by James W. Baker, who was director of research at the Plimoth Plantation for many years. Rather than dealing with the myths surrounding the Pilgrims, Baker sought to get at what he called the holiday's theological roots. He agreed with Love that the 1621 feast was not an orthodox Puritan Thanksgiving, unlike the one on July 30, 1623. The author pointed out that it was not until the mid-nineteenth century that the Pilgrims were even associated with Thanksgiving by the general public. When Sarah Josepha Hale started to promote the holiday in *Godey's Lady's Book* in 1837, there was little mention of the Pilgrims. Baker also felt that Thanksgiving became "feminized" and domesticated under Hale and others and served to replace the more "masculine" observance of Forefathers Day, or December 22nd, the anniversary of their landing in the new world.

Much of the book was devoted to the "selling and marketing" of Thanksgiving through literature, novels and poetry, art, schoolbooks and activities, greetings cards, advertising, and much else. It was pointed out that often paintings, that are anachronistic or inaccurate in other ways, have a major impact on what people know or believe; an example was the Jennie Brownscombe 1914 painting, which showed a log cabin and Native

Americans with Plains Indian headdresses. As a member of the Plantation staff, Baker had been involved in the production of a *Thanksgiving Primer*, which treated the 1621 event as only a harvest festival. He has also witnessed the demonstrations by Native American groups since 1970 against the day of Thanksgiving, calling it a "Day of Mourning." According to Baker, a new myth, glorifying the Indians and defaming the Pilgrims, has been created in place of the old.

Kirkpatrick's Thanksgiving: The Holiday at the Heart of the American Experience

In her 2016 history of Thanksgiving Day, Melanie Kirkpatrick has correctly recognized the 1621 three-day event of the Pilgrims and their Wampanoag guests as a harvest festival, not an official Thanksgiving, but she has also quoted from Love's book in accepting it as the forerunner of the beloved holiday we know today. She has also expounded in greater detail on other claims to be the "First Thanksgiving" in North America and has spelled out the work of Sarah Josepha Hale, whom she called the "Godmother of Thanksgiving." Kirkpatrick has brought the history up to date with the tradition of football games, Roosevelt's changing of the date, protests by Native Americans, and the tradition of charitable giving. She did not call it a patriotic holiday, but one that expresses patriotic feelings of gratitude for national blessings of civil and religious liberty. What was delightful about the book were the "Readings for Thanksgiving" by noted authors and many recipes for traditional food.

The Thanksgiving Primer and 1621: A New Look at Thanksgiving

Both were products of the Plimouth Plantation, which was chartered in 1947 to re-create the original Plymouth settlement. The booklets call the 1621 event a harvest festival, and the *Primer* stated that the modern American Thanksgiving evolved from a merger of three traditions, English harvest home, Puritan religious service, and Forefathers Day.

Antecedents of the Holiday

Appelbaum wrote that the mother and father of Thanksgiving were the Connecticut and Plymouth colonies, while the four "grandparents" or traditions from the old world were: Harvest Home; Christmas; Civil Proclamations; and Religious Proclamations. Baker believed that the holiday was a synthesis of three independent traditions: Calvinist Thanksgiving; English harvest festival; and Forefathers Day. It could be argued that there were four antecedents of the Pilgrim Thanksgiving: 1) the Hebrew harvest festival, recorded in the Book of Deuteronomy; 2) the English Harvest Home; 3) the Puritan Thanksgiving; 4) the Dutch day of commemoration.

Hebrew Harvest Festival

In his 1987 Doctor of Ministry thesis at Hartford Seminary William J. Zito wrote about "Thanksgiving Day: Deepening and Strengthening the Secular and the Holy." He pointed out that the practice of thanksgiving was indigenous to Judaism, with three major festivals. One was Passover or Pesach, which was a festival of thanksgiving for deliverance from bondage in Egypt. Contemporary observances of Passover are very powerful symbolic acts, with each person vicariously reliving the history of a people gaining freedom. A second was the Festival of Weeks or Shavuot, established to commemorate the day when God revealed himself to Moses on Mt. Sinai. It is also called Pentecost or the Festival of the First Fruits. The third is the Feast of Tabernacles or Sukkoth, which celebrated the ingathering of the harvest. This was observed by the construction of temporary shelters or booths to remember the forty years of wandering in the wilderness.

When people brought forth the first fruits of the harvest, they intoned what scholars call one of the oldest statements or confessions of faith in the Bible, found in the Book of Deuteronomy, chapter 26: verses 5–9. In a more recent English translation, it began: "A wandering Aramean was my ancestor." The Aramean was Jacob, whose descendants sojourned in the land of Egypt, were oppressed, cried to the Lord in their distress, were liberated from bondage under Moses and brought over the sea and through the wilderness to a new land, flowing with milk and honey. The Hebrew word for "wandering" did not mean nomadic, but rather one who is "in danger of perishing." The two most important parts of the statement were that God had saved them and that they had received land.

The English translation that the Pilgrims brought with them to the new world was the Geneva Bible of 1565, and the verses from Deuteronomy read:

> "A Syrian was my father, who being ready to perish for hunger, went down into Egypt, and sojourned there with a small company, and grew there into a nation great, mighty and full of people . . . And the Lord brought us out of Egypt, and he hath brought us into this place and hath given us this land, even a land that floweth with milk and honey."[5]

When Bradford wrote his history of the Plymouth Plantation, he described their first landfall: "they fell upon their knees and blessed the God of Heaven." He remembered the ancient statement of faith from the Hebrew harvest festival and expressed his own faith that God had acted in their history in this way:

> "Our fathers were Englishmen, which came over this great ocean, and were ready to perish in this wilderness; but they cried unto the Lord, and He heard their voice and looked on their adversity. Let them therefore praise the Lord, because He is good, and His mercies endure forever."[6]

The meaning of this quote from Bradford has been overlooked in the various treatments of the subject. These Pilgrim fathers and mothers used the biblical story to tell their own story. Like the Israelites of old, they felt guided by God to leave the tyranny and oppression of the past and cross a sea to what was called a promised land. According to Jon Meacham in *American Gospel,* Thomas Jefferson proposed that the Great Seal of the new country show the Israelites "in the wilderness led by a cloud by day and a pillar of fire by night."

English Harvest Home

According to the Lintons, the completing of the harvest in the English countryside was a festive occasion. The last wagon of grain was greeted by people with flowers and ribbons, with cheers and singing. Depending upon the village, the one who cut the last sheaf of wheat was called the "lord of the harvest," and a girl clothed in white would ride on top of the wagon

5. Deut 26:5, 7 (*Geneva Bible*)
6. Bradford, Ibid. 63

as the "Queen of the Harvest." After everything was stored in barns, they would sit down to a harvest home supper.

As recently as the nineteenth century, there was even a hymn written, which begins: "Come, ye thankful people come, Raise the song of harvest home." Robert Herrick wrote a poem, describing the festivities in seventeenth century England, called "The Hock Cart or Harvest Home" which began:

> "Come, Sons of summer, by whose toil
> We are the lords of wine and oil;
> By whose tough labours and rough hands,
> We rip up first, then reap our lands.
> Crown'd with the ears of corn, now come,
> And, to the pipe, sing Harvest Home!"[7]

The Pilgrims brought this tradition with them to the New World. Even though they had little or no opportunity for farming in Leiden, the Netherlands, they did not leave their English customs in the ocean on the way over.

The time of harvest in the Plymouth colony was of critical importance. Winslow's letter to a friend in England mentioned the harvest, but Bradford went into more detail in his history:

> "They began now to gather in the small harvest they had, and to fit up their houses and dwellings against winter, being all well recovered in health and strength, and had all things in good plenty. For as some were thus employed in affairs abroad, others were exercised in fishing, about cod and bass and other fish, of which they took good store, of which every family had their portion. All the summer there was no want, and now began to come in store of fowl, as winter approached, of which this place did abound when they came first . . . And besides waterfowl there was great store of wild turkeys, of which they took many, besides venison, etc. Besides they had about a peck of meal a week to a person, or now since harvest, Indian corn to that proportion."[8]

Bradford's history and Winslow's letter have convinced scholars that the Pilgrims and their Native American visitors enjoyed a three-day harvest festival in 1621.

7. Linton, *We Gather Together*, 37
8. Bradford, Ibid, 90

Puritan Thanksgiving

Contrary to Hodgson's assertion, the Pilgrims were a part of the Separatist wing of the Puritan movement. And contrary to Appelbaum, they were not "religious fanatics." Puritans felt that the Church of England did not go far enough in getting rid of what were considered "popish" elements and wanted to "purify" the church. They opposed bishops and archbishops, clerical vestments, kneeling at communion, use of the ring in weddings, and other practices. They did not recognize the many saints' days or celebrate Christmas and Easter, because they were not in the Bible. The only day set aside on a regular basis was the Sabbath.

These Separatists, who did not want to remain in communion with the Church of England, formed a congregation in Scrooby, England, with John Robinson as their pastor. They believed in the autonomy of the local congregation as a "covenanted community" and felt that only the local congregation could call and ordain their own ministers and set aside days of fasting or thanksgiving. Because of their views, they were hunted, harassed, arrested, and some were jailed. They decided to leave England and go to the Netherlands, which had become a refuge for persecuted people.

After several false starts and disappointments, they fled to Amsterdam, where there already were English congregations, and then to the city of Leiden. After nearly twelve years some members of the congregation decided to leave for the New World, but their pastor, John Robinson, did not make the trip. He had taught his congregation that God exercises a providential care over people in ordering events, and therefore prayer and thanksgiving were appropriate responses, either in private or public. Both prayer and thanksgiving preceded the decision to depart by boat for the new world. There were some French Huguenots who joined the "Saints" for the voyage and also "Strangers" or non-Separatists, hired men and indentured servants. (The voyage was paid for by a group of London merchant adventurers, and the Pilgrims' relationship with them was very difficult, because of the requirement to pay back the loan with a portion of their earnings in seven years.)

The days of Fast or Thanksgiving set aside by these Separatists included a religious service with long sermons, prayers and the singing of Psalms. In July 1623 the Pilgrims set aside days for both fasting and feasting. In that year the Plymouth colony was in danger of collapsing; they were running out of food and supplies, there was a drought, and their crops were not growing. Bradford wrote: "Upon which they set apart a solemn day of humiliation, to seek the Lord by humble and fervent prayer, in this great distress." Several things happened. Miles Standish was able to buy supplies from a Scottish trader; three ships came to the colony, including some people from the congregation in Leiden, and the rain came. They set apart a day of thanksgiving, which was celebrated on July 30, according to Love's research. This was the Pilgrims' first real Thanksgiving Day.

Dutch Day of Commemoration, or "Herdenking"

The Lintons referred to Dutch days of prayer and thanksgiving "to commemorate military victories and other special events." Appelbaum wrote about the important day of October 3rd, when the Dutch celebrated independence from the Spanish empire. Actually the "Third of October" was celebrated each year in the city of Leiden to commemorate the lifting of the siege by the Spanish army in 1574, and the Pilgrims shared in this during their nearly twelve years of residence in that city.

In 1574 the Spanish army laid siege to the important, but heavily armed and walled city of Leiden. For four months the city held out and would not surrender, although many died of starvation and disease. Elsewhere in the country Dutch soldiers and sailors worked to save the city. Dikes were broken in many places to allow the waters of the North Sea to flow over the land, and finally the night of October 2nd, the Dutch sailors, called "water beggars," brought their boats to the city and drove the Spanish away. They also brought white bread and herring fish to feed the population, and a boy ventured outside the city and found "hutspot," a kind of stew at an abandoned Spanish campsite. These foods were incorporated in the annual day of commemoration. On October 3rd the Dutch admiral led the people to the Peter's Church, where they joined in prayers and hymns of thanksgiving. It was recorded that they could not finish the hymn because of the weeping.

The saving of the Plymouth colony in 1623 could be compared to the lifting of the siege of the city of Leiden, and it called for equally fervent prayer and thanksgiving. Bradford wrote: "And afterwards the Lord sent them such seasonable showers, with interchange of fair warm weather as, through His blessing caused a fruitful and liberal harvest, to their no small comfort and rejoicing. For which mercy, in time convenient, they also set apart a day of thanksgiving."[9]

9. Ibid, 131–32

Thanksgiving goes national

Thanksgiving days have been changed, contested, and cancelled. The story is told that in 1705 the town of Colchester, Connecticut, postponed the holiday because a shipment of molasses was delayed and the people weren't able to make pumpkin pies! At the end of that century Thanksgiving became an issue of partisan politics. The Federalist-leaning clergy and the Jeffersonian-affiliated government officials argued over the matter as to who had the authority to proclaim the holiday. Before the Civil War some clergy in northern states used the holiday to voice their abolitionist views, and southern states refused to recognize what they deemed a "Yankee holiday."

While Connecticut and Massachusetts, and later New Hampshire, celebrated an annual Thanksgiving Day in November, the other colonies continued the practice of setting aside such days for special occasions and events. The first national day was proclaimed by the Continental Congress in 1777 after the American victory in Saratoga, New York, in the Revolutionary War.

When the first U.S. Congress met in 1789 in New York City, there was a debate about whether a national Thanksgiving Day should be inaugurated. It resulted in two proclamations, while George Washington was President, one in 1789 to give thanks for the new Constitution and its implementation. The other proclamation was in 1795 to give thanks for the suppression of the "whiskey rebellion" in western Pennsylvania. The last President to proclaim a day of Thanksgiving before Lincoln was James Madison, who in 1815 expressed gratitude for the Treaty of Ghent, ending the War of 1812.

Much of the credit for the annual proclamation of a national Thanksgiving Day in November goes to Sarah Josepha Hale. There were others who wrote poetry, stories and even novels that dealt with the New England custom, but it was Hale who editorialized about it in her magazine, and wrote to governors and U.S. Presidents to have the day established by law. Sarah Josepha Buell was born in Newport, New Hampshire, in 1788. Educated by her mother and her brother, who went to Dartmouth College, she taught school when she was eighteen, and began to write poetry and other works. Among her poems was the well-known "Mary had a little lamb." She married David Hale, an attorney, in 1813, and the couple had five children, but her husband died in 1822.

With support from her late husband's Masonic lodge she published a book of poetry, but her novel, *Northwood: or Life North and South*, or *A New England Tale*, brought her to the attention of a minister, who recruited her to be the editor of the *Ladies' Magazine*, headquartered in Boston. When the magazine was merged with *Godey's Lady's Book* in 1837 she became the editor and moved to Philadelphia. She continued as editor for forty years, and the magazine became very successful. She was a strong advocate for the education of women, the abolition of slavery, and preservation of the Union. She also raised money to build the Bunker Hill monument, holding a craft fair at Quincy Market in Boston, and she supported the preservation of Washington's home at Mt. Vernon. She also helped to establish Vassar College and a women's hospital in Philadelphia.

Each year in the November issue of her magazine, she wrote about making Thanksgiving a day of national festivity. In the sixth chapter of her novel, *Northwood*, a New England family entertained a guest from England on the day before Thanksgiving, and he wanted to know the meaning of the holiday. It is curious that the author did not mention the 1621 harvest festival, but does allude to the "providential manner," when an official Fast Day turned to Thanksgiving in 1623, but she placed the "pilgrim band" in the wrong colony, Boston, instead of Plymouth! The English guest is told that "it is considered as an appropriate tribute of gratitude to God to set apart one day of Thanksgiving in each year, and autumn is the time when the overflowing garners of America call for the expression of joyful gratitude." When asked if this is a national holiday, the English guest is told that it is not but will become one. "We have too few holidays. Thanksgiving, like the Fourth of July, should be considered a national festival and observed by all our people . . . as an exponent of our Republican institutions, which are based on the acknowledgment that God is our Lord and that, as a nation, we derive our privileges and blessings from Him."[10]

Besides editorials in her magazine, she included stories, recipes, poems and pictures, even ideas for decorating the house. She has been called an "arbiter of taste," and a kind of Oprah and Martha Stewart! Besides campaigning in her magazine, she wrote to the governors of all the states and to five U.S. Presidents, urging them to proclaim an official holiday. She reported in 1859 that thirty states and three territories held Thanksgiving on the same day, the last Thursday of November. Abraham Lincoln was the first President to respond to her appeal. On October 26, 1863, he issued a proclamation to have all Americans "set apart and observe the last Thursday of November next, as a day of Thanksgiving and Praise to our beneficent

10. Hale, *Northwood*, 67–68

Father who dwelleth in the Heavens."[11] In doing so Lincoln inaugurated a custom that has continued to the present day.

Annual Thanksgiving Days were at one time characterized by a long church service in the morning followed by dinner and another service in the afternoon. Appelbaum reported that the dinner became so popular and elaborate that the afternoon or evening service was suspended. Through the years the religious component waned, but there were other changes as well. In the early years of the country the holiday was associated with a wintry scene, hence the trip to grandfather's house in a sleigh; by the end of the nineteenth century Thanksgiving was bedecked with the colors of autumn. In the early years the dinner was followed by games, sports, dances, and even hunting and a turkey shoot; again, before the twentieth century dawned, championship football games were on the menu, and later came parades. The holiday also grew as a major time of homecoming and family reunions, and became the most traveled time of the year. One of the most important changes was that it spread from New England to all parts of the country, thanks in great part to Sarah Josepha Hale.

Conclusion

Several things are worth reiterating and emphasizing. The Pilgrims' Thanksgiving was not the first act or ritual of thanksgiving in the new world. However, not only did it capture the imagination of the American people, but it brought together elements from at least four traditions of the past and bequeathed to future generations a legacy that had a wealth of meanings. It is true that the 1621 event with the Pilgrims and their Native American visitors was more of a harvest festival, but it needs to be set in the context of the total "Pilgrim experience." This included the 1620 landfall and Bradford's reference to the confession of faith intoned by the Israelites at one of their harvest festivals, and the July 30, 1623, Day of Thanksgiving after a very difficult year when the little colony was in danger of perishing.

It is foolish to call the "First Thanksgiving of the Pilgrims" a myth or pious fiction because they didn't have cranberry sauce or pumpkin pie or even roast turkey on the menu. The fact that their three-day festival has stood the test of time speaks volumes about their faith and fortitude and that of their descendants who wanted to honor them. The fact is that these were real human beings, not cardboard cut-outs, painted figures, or plaster

11. Lincoln, *Speeches and Writings*, Vol. 2:520–21

saints. As articulated by later settlers of Massachusetts Bay Colony, they were a "new Israel," an "errand in the wilderness," "a city set upon a hill," a "chosen people" with a special mission and destiny in the world.

The problem is that Thanksgiving, as it is generally celebrated, is incomplete.

- It is observed as a purely *secular* holiday but it has a *spiritual* or *religious* dimension. Which raises the question: To whom or what are we directing our thanksgiving? One American history book suggested that the Pilgrims were giving thanks to the Native Americans. The purpose of Thanksgiving, going back to biblical times, was to thank God for his benevolence, mercy and grace, for his mighty deeds in history.

- It is observed as a *private* or *personal* family meal, but it has a *public* face. Since colonial times proclamations have called for "A Day of Public Thanksgiving." It is a time to celebrate in inter-faith and ecumenical services.

- It is observed as a *harvest festival,* but it invites us to *prayer and thanksgiving.* The great majority of Americans do not live on farms and do not grow their own food, so the meal provides an opportunity to think about all the people, including migrant workers, who do the backbreaking work in the hot sun, and those who toil in the canneries, plants, markets, and elsewhere, so that we will have food on the table, and the God who provides.

- It is observed as a *nuclear or extended family* event, but it needs the *national* and *historical* context, since it affords an opportunity to give thanks to God for the blessings of liberty, as one of the high holy days of American civil or public religion.

- It is observed with some degree of *excess* and *consumption*, but the historic traditions of the holiday include the element of *sharing*—with those in need and the less fortunate, the lonely, the elderly, the strangers and newcomers in our midst.

On the wall of the meeting room of the Cheshire Historical Society (Connecticut) is an original, framed print of the Thanksgiving Proclamation in 1834 by the Governor, Samuel A. Foot of Cheshire. His reference to "The Pilgrims and their descendants" indicated that the association of Thanksgiving with the Plymouth Colony went back earlier than commonly believed. The Governor called for a day of "public *Thanksgiving, Prayer, And Praise To*

Almighty God," and invited citizens to gather "at their usual places of religious worship." In doing so he followed a custom that was begun in the seventeenth century. This tradition of annual proclamations was the oldest in the country and was proudly continued in the twentieth century with some of the most beautiful ever written, the ones by Wilbur Cross, which was not surprising since he had been a professor of English at Yale University and Dean of the Graduate School before he was elected governor. In his call for a "A Day of Public Thanksgiving" in 1937 the governor wrote:

> "Let us then, as our fathers used, praise the Giver of Life for the ample fruit of the earth, sweetened by sun and rain, and for the work of the laborer worthy of his hire in every task and station: for food and clothing and shelter that serve the body's need. Let us praise Him especially for the blessings which have warmed and fostered the spirit: for every brave, just, and generous deed, every impulse of brotherly love; for every counsel of wisdom and comfort, every witness of truth, every thought of friends who walk with us still, though lost to our sight—for all the tokens of goodness in man, which have deepened faith in our power, looking within the hearts, to fix our eyes upon virtue as upon the Pole Star, and by it keep our way to the mortal end. For these mercies, without name or number, let us rejoice and give praise."[12]

12. A Proclamation by Governor Wilbur L. Cross, (November 9, 1937)

He Belongs to the Ages

ABRAHAM LINCOLN'S BIRTHDAY

ON THE BICENTENNIAL OF the birth of Abraham Lincoln, there was a flurry of publications about the sixteenth president of the United States. In reality, there has never been a let up of Lincoln studies. More biographical material has been published about him than any other American: over 16,000 and counting. He has been considered the greatest of American Presidents, an American icon, a part of the national pantheon, the savior of the Union, the second founder of the nation, a martyr, or even a "Christ figure." There is endless fascination with his life and career and a never-ending debate over the complexities and contradictions of his personality and policies. Lincoln has been enshrined in the temple-like memorial in Washington, DC, chiseled on Mount Rushmore, engraved on the nation's coins and currency, and his Gettysburg Address and Second Inaugural Address have been added to the sacred texts of the American civil or public religion. In time for the bicentennial the Lincoln penny was redesigned, and a set of four postage stamps was issued, depicting scenes in his life. Lincoln's birthday has been celebrated in some states, but it has never been a federal holiday. Recently, there was an unsuccessful attempt in the U.S. Congress to combine it with Washington's Birthday on the third Monday of February.

In the bicentennial year of his birth there was even more interest because of the inauguration of another tall, slim lawyer from Illinois as the forty-fourth president, Barack Obama: the train trip from Philadelphia to Washington, DC; the program in front of the Lincoln Memorial; the use of the Lincoln Bible for the swearing-in ceremony.

While Lincoln was still living, there were brief autobiographies and longer campaign biographies. The editor of the *New York Times*, Henry Raymond, compiled such a biography and, after Lincoln's assassination, it was re-published with a chapter on his death and entitled *The Life and Public Service of Abraham Lincoln*. My great grandmother, Mary Irene (Dixon) Wardell, who lived in Georgetown, purchased a copy and it has been handed down in my family for generations. It was in my mother's library, along with the volumes by Carl Sandburg, *The Prairie Years* and *The War Years*; the book, *Lincoln's Devotional*; another book, *The Soul of Abraham Lincoln* by William E. Barton; and a biography, *Lincoln the President: Midstream*, by J.G. Randall.

Many aspects of his life, career, and character have been examined. There have been books on his young adulthood, his marriage, his wife's family, his legal and political career, the Lincoln-Douglas debates, his attitudes toward slavery, his cabinet (called by historian Doris Kearns Goodwin a "team of rivals"), the conduct of the war and the relationship with his generals, his "other White House," his letters and public addresses, his relevance for today. Allen C. Guelzo has written what he calls an "intellectual biography," William Lee Miller an "ethical biography," Ronald C. White, Jr. a kind of "rhetorical biography," Michael Burlingame a "psycho-biography," Joshua W. Shenk on Lincoln's melancholy.

The two generations after Lincoln's death saw the publication of the collected reminiscences by his law partner, William Herndon, and the recollections of his White House secretaries, John Hay and John Nicolay. Two major events in the twentieth century opened the door for extensive research. One was the release of the Robert Todd Lincoln papers in 1947, and the other was the publication of the nine-volume writings of Lincoln by Rutgers University Press in 1953, edited by Roy Basler. The biography by Benjamin P. Thomas in 1952, simply entitled *Abraham Lincoln,* has been regarded as one of the best one-volume treatments. A generation later came a biography by Stephen B. Oates, *With Malice Toward None: The Life of Abraham Lincoln*. More recently, David Herbert Donald has won the Lincoln Prize for his work on Lincoln, notably the 1995 biography, *Lincoln*. A British scholar, Richard Carwardine, has also received the Lincoln prize for his book, *Lincoln: A Life of Purpose and Power*. In time for the bicentennial came the two volumes by Burlingame, *Abraham Lincoln: A Life and* a new book by White, *A. Lincoln: A Biography*.

Three years after the birthday bicentennial Stephen Spielberg released his award-winning movie, *Lincoln*, with Daniel Day Lewis playing the part of the President and Sally Field as his wife. A virtue of the film was the decision to limit its focus to the last months of Lincoln's life, the struggle to end the Civil War, and the battle in the U.S. Congress to pass the Thirteenth Amendment outlawing slavery. Tony Kushner's screenplay drew upon Goodwin's book, *Team of Rivals*, as a resource and portrayed the leadership skills of Lincoln as he bartered and bargained for votes. The film was true to Lincoln's difficult relationship with his wife and his fatherly care for his two remaining sons, Tad and Robert. Most stirring were the Union soldiers reciting parts of the Gettysburg Address at the beginning and Lincoln delivering his Second Inaugural Address at the end.

Lincoln's Autobiography

Unlike George Washington, Lincoln actually penned an autobiography, not once but twice, but very reluctantly and briefly. In 1858 Jesse Fell, a friend and secretary of the Illinois state Republican Committee, asked Lincoln to write about his life. Lincoln's original response was that "there is nothing in my early history that would interest you or anybody else." A year later Fell was given a short piece that took up several paragraphs and only 606 words. After Lincoln was nominated to be President of the United States by the Republican National Convention in Chicago in 1860, the editor of the *Chicago Press and Tribune* asked Lincoln to write about his life as the basis for a campaign biography. The candidate told the editor, John L. Scripps: "It is a great piece of folly to attempt to make anything out of my early life." Lincoln quoted from "Elegy Written in a Country Churchyard," by Thomas Gray: "The short and simple annals of the poor. That's my life and that's all you or anyone else can make of it."

On June 1, 1860, Lincoln did provide the editor with a somewhat longer autobiography, but entirely in the third person, referring to himself as "A," "Mr. L" or the "subject." He said he was born on February 12, 1809, in Hardin County, Kentucky, and that his parents were of undistinguished families. His father and grandfather had moved to Kentucky from Virginia, and the family was originally of the Quaker tradition. His grandfather was killed by Indians in 1784 while working on the farm, and his father grew up without a father or an education. Lincoln's father married Nancy Hanks in 1806, and they had two children; his older sister died in childbirth after she had married. Lincoln said that he had little formal education, amounting to a year or so, but he learned how to read and write and "cipher." Lincoln wrote that he had "picked up" learning from time to time under the pressure of necessity. He read many books which he borrowed from other people. In his autobiography Lincoln never mentioned the names of the books, which included Bunyan's *Pilgrim's Progress,* Aesop's *Fables,* the life of Washington, the history of the United States, the King James Bible, and many others.

The family moved to Indiana in 1816 to get away from slavery and difficulty with land titles. They faced the formidable task of clearing a forest, and Lincoln wrote about having an axe put in his hands at a young age in order to fell the trees. His father worked him very hard and even farmed him out as a hired hand to other neighbors. His mother died in 1818, and a year later his father married Sally Johnston, a widow with three children. When Lincoln was nineteen years old, he made the first of two boat trips down the river to New Orleans to deliver livestock and produce.

In 1830 the family moved again, this time to Illinois, and Lincoln helped to build a log cabin and split many rails to serve as fencing. At age twenty-one he left the family to live in New Salem, where he had a job as a clerk. The business failed and he contemplated the blacksmith trade, but learned the art of surveying. However, he acquired another store and became the postmaster. He joined a volunteer company in the Black Hawk War, was elected captain, but saw no action. Lincoln also ran for the state legislature in 1832, but lost the election; he wrote that it was the only time in his life when he ever was beaten in a direct vote by the people. (He was a candidate for the U.S. Senate twice in the 1850s, but in those days the state legislatures chose the Senators.)

Lincoln ran again and was elected to the state legislature in 1834, and was re-elected three times. It is not mentioned in his autobiography that he was involved in the decision to move the Illinois state capital from Vandalia to Springfield. In the legislature he met an attorney, John Stuart, who encouraged him to study law. Borrowing law books from Stuart, Lincoln received a law license in 1836, moved to Springfield the following year, and became a partner with his mentor. The young lawyer was a member of the Whig party and served three times as a member of the Electoral College, for William Henry Harrison in 1840, Henry Clay in 1844, and Winfield Scott in 1852. He was elected to the U.S. House of Representatives in 1846, and voted for supplies for the American troops in the Mexican War, but strongly opposed the war. Lincoln had married Mary Todd of Lexington,

Kentucky, and the couple had four boys. He does not mention the death of their son Eddie in 1850.

After one term in the U.S. Congress he devoted himself to the practice of law, but the repeal of the Missouri Compromise in 1854 "aroused him as he had never been before." Early in his life he had found the system of slavery to be wrong, and his opinion never changed. He does not mention the speech he gave in Springfield on June 16, 1858, at the close of the state Republican convention, which nominated him to be a U.S. Senator. It was famous because of the statement, "A house divided against itself cannot stand. I believe this government cannot endure, permanently half slave and half free." Nor does he mention the seven debates he had with the Democrat Party nominee, the incumbent Stephen Douglas, all over the state of Illinois from Aug. 21 through October 15, 1858. Also omitted is his trip to the East, his lectures in New England, and his famous talk at Cooper Union in New York City on February 27, 1860.

After mentioning his reaction to the repeal of the Missouri Compromise, he concluded his 1859 piece by saying: "What I have done since then is pretty well known." However, he did add a personal description: that he was six feet, four inches tall, weighed on average 180 pounds, had a dark complexion, with coarse dark hair and grey eyes. That was the end of his 1860 autobiography.

It could be said that what happened in the last five years of his life is very well known. On November 6, 1860, Lincoln was elected President with almost forty percent of the popular vote (three other candidates split the remaining votes) and 180 of the 303 electoral votes. South Carolina seceded from the Union on December 20, and it was followed by ten other southern states, which formed a new country, the Confederate States of America. He bid "an affectionate farewell" to the citizens of his hometown, Springfield, on February 11, and traveled by train to Washington, DC, delivering speeches on the way in Indiana, Ohio, Pennsylvania, New York, and New Jersey. He completed the choices for his cabinet, including former contenders for the Republican nomination as President, and was inaugurated on March 4, 1861, before a partially built national Capitol building.

His administration was almost entirely consumed by the Civil War and his constitutional duty as Commander in Chief. A month after his inauguration, Fort Sumter was fired on by Confederate forces, and the garrison surrendered two days later. Six days after the surrender of General Robert E. Lee at Appomattox Court House, Lincoln died as a result of being shot at Ford's Theatre by John Wilkes Booth. The intervening years were consumed by Union defeats and victories, a series of Union generals, concluding with Ulysses S. Grant and Sherman's conquest of Atlanta and march to the sea. In the second year of his presidency the Lincolns lost another son, Willie, from which his wife Mary never recovered.

Most memorable during these years were his brief but brilliant address at the dedication of the Gettysburg military cemetery, the issuing of the Emancipation Proclamation, which went into effect on January 1, 1863, and his Second Inaugural Address. Lincoln was re-elected to a second term as President on November 8, 1864, with fifty-five percent of the popular vote and 212 of 233 electoral votes. He defeated General George McClellan, the nominee of the Democratic Party, and was inaugurated on March 4, 1865. His Second Inaugural Address, as well as his Gettysburg Address, are inscribed on the walls of the Lincoln Memorial.

Because of the horrendous Civil War it is easy to forget the other accomplishments of the Lincoln administration. The sixteenth President came to the office with a Whig Party background and commitment to internal improvements and an expanded infrastructure. Each December Lincoln would send an annual message to the Congress, which was read by the clerk. The thirty-seventh Congress was one of the most productive in American history. In its three sessions the Congress passed the following measures: the abolition of slavery in the District of Columbia; establishment of the Department of Agriculture; the Homestead Act; the Pacific Railway Act, leading to the building of the trans-continental railroad; the Land Grant Colleges Act; and the National Banking Act. Lincoln worked with the thirty-eighth Congress to pass the Thirteenth Amendment to the Constitution, abolishing slavery. Before his death he had tried to set in motion terms of amnesty, reunion, and reconciliation that would restore the southern states to the Union. Unfortunately, the period of Reconstruction after the war was a failure in many respects, which leads one to wonder what would have happened if Lincoln were able to complete his second term.

Conclusion

When Lincoln died the morning of April 15th in a house across the street from Ford's Theatre, the Secretary of War, Edwin Stanton, uttered the immortal words, "Now, he belongs to the ages." Now, Lincoln belongs to the

American people, all the people, North and South, East and West. Lincoln's humble beginnings and extraordinary life have endeared him to the American people, and there was a great outpouring of mourning for the fallen President as his funeral train took him back to the state of Illinois.

I wrote an article, "Lincoln's Birthday Should Be a Federal Holiday," which was published in the winter 2015 issue of the newsletter, *For the People,* of the Abraham Lincoln Association. In it I listed at least seven reasons why a federal holiday should be declared.

1. Lincoln is considered one of the greatest Presidents in American history, if not the greatest.

2. The sixteenth President provided the indispensable leadership to save the Union.

3. He led the fight to abolish slavery, a cruel institution which ran counter to all American ideals of freedom, equality, and justice.

4. Two of the most significant pieces of American literature were contributed by Lincoln, the Gettysburg Address and the Second Inaugural Address.

5. He was the main exemplar and proponent of American civil or public religion, what Lincoln called "political religion."

6. In his speeches he reclaimed the founding documents of the country, recounting that all men were created equal and endowed by their creator with life, liberty, and the pursuit of happiness.

7. The Lincoln Memorial anchors the western end of the National Mall, one of only two monuments to American Presidents on the country's "back yard."

It is true that Lincoln's Birthday has never been a federal holiday, but the fact that it is celebrated in seven states and added to Presidents' Day in other states indicates that Lincoln was more than just the favorite son of Illinois. Washington's Birthday should be restored to its original date, and Lincoln's Birthday added to the civil calendar, so that the entire nation can join in honoring its two most important chief executives, one who helped to create this great country and the other one who saved it.

APPENDIX B

Leaders of Labor

LABOR DAY

IT IS UNFORTUNATE THAT the term, "labor leader" has become a pejorative one, because the labor movement was indebted to a number of visionary people who provided leadership through the very difficult years of struggle to secure higher wages, more reasonable working hours, and better working conditions for the men and women in what was called the "rank and file." These men and women rose up from the ranks and fifteen of them were included in a 1987 book edited by Dubofsky and Van Tine, *Labor Leaders in America*. Mother Jones has been added to the list, not so much because of her official capacity but because of her unfailing advocacy of the cause of working people. These leaders came from different ethnic, religious, and philosophical backgrounds, and held different occupations. Five of them were born in other countries. One ran five times for President of the United States as a candidate of the Socialist Party. Several brought radical ideas from the international labor movement, undergirded by Marxism, while others were home-grown in their viewpoints. At least two were members of the Communist Party for a time, while others were fiercely anti-Communist. Two taught a Sunday school class in churches, and one was greatly influenced by the Social Gospel movement.

William Sylvis (1828–1869) grew up in western Pennsylvania, but moved to Philadelphia after his marriage. A pioneering labor leader, Sylvis helped to organize the National Union of Iron Molders and was elected president of the National Labor Union in 1868. In this capacity he worked to include women and African-Americans, and was a friend of Susan B. Anthony. He led the battle for the eight-hour work day and called for the creation of a national labor party. Sylvis taught a Sunday school class in a Methodist church in Philadelphia.

Mary Harris "Mother" Jones (1837–1930) was born in Ireland and came with her family to Canada and then to this country in 1860. She married George E. Jones and bore four children, but she lost her husband and all her children in an epidemic in Memphis in 1878. Mary Harris Jones worked as a dressmaker in Chicago and joined the Knights of Labor. As an organizer for the United Mine Workers, she traveled widely and supported strikers in West Virginia, New Jersey, Pennsylvania, Colorado, and elsewhere. After the "Ludlow massacre" she met with John D. Rockefeller, Jr. in New York City to air grievances and seek restitution.

Terence Powderly (1849–1924) grew up in northeastern Pennsylvania in the anthracite coal country, and began work on the Delaware and Hudson Railroad and joined the Machinists Union in 1872. It was said that his views on economic, social and political issues had a strong moral and religious foundation. He believed that all work was holy and noble and the source of human happiness, but he was in favor of abolishing the wage system. He was elected mayor of Scranton in 1878, and from 1879 to 1893 was the head of the Knights of Labor. In 1885 he led a successful strike against the Southwestern Railroad of Jay Gould.

Samuel Gompers (1850–1924) was born in London, England, and came to New York City in 1863. A cigar maker by occupation, Gompers was influenced by Marxism and the First International and identified with the Marxist view of the class struggle. However, he became more conservative and adopted the American approach to the political process. He was a member of the Cigarmakers Union and worked for high dues and good benefits, but he was opposed to industrial or unskilled unionism. For nearly thirty-eight years he was the head of the American Federation of Labor, which he had helped to organize in 1886.

Eugene Debs (1855–1926) grew up in Terre Haute, Indiana, began work on the railroads and became a charter member of the Brotherhood of Locomotive Firemen. He was elected city clerk in Terre Haute and also won election to the Indiana state legislature. Debs helped to organize the American Railway Union and led the Pullman strike of 1894. Through his own experiences and reading he became a committed socialist and ran five times from 1900 to 1920 (the last time from prison) for U.S. President as the candidate of the Socialist Party.

William D. "Big Bill" Haywood (1869–1928) was born in Salt Lake City, left home early to work as a miner in Nevada and Idaho, and became a member of the Western Federation of Miners. He survived the violent strikes at Cripple Creek and Telluride, Colorado. As a member of the Socialist Party, he attended a conference of the Second International in Copenhagen and was dedicated to changing the system of capitalism. In 1905 he helped to organize the Industrial Workers of the World and served as its President. Among other events, he was a leader in the "Bread and Roses" strike in Lawrence, Massachusetts. Opposed to the First World War and arrested on account of the Espionage Act of 1917, Haywood went to the Soviet Union, where he died.

William Green (1870–1952) was born in Coshocton, Ohio, in a devout Baptist family. He was profoundly influenced by the Social Gospel movement and considered becoming a minister. He did teach a Sunday school class in a Baptist church, and at age seventeen he became a miner and later an officer of the Progressive Miners Union and the United Mine Workers. As an Ohio state senator, he helped the legislature pass a workers' compensation law. Green became vice president of the American Federation of Labor in 1913 and President in 1924.

John L. Lewis (1880–1969) grew up in Iowa and worked as a miner in Iowa and Illinois. He became a full-time paid AFL organizer and by 1920 had been elected president of the United Mine Workers. Lewis supported the "New Deal" policies of Roosevelt and was appointed to the labor advisory board of the National Recovery Administration, but opposed Roosevelt's election for a third term in 1940. Lewis was a strong supporter of industrial unionism and helped to organize the Congress of Industrial Organizations in 1935, becoming president. He resigned as head of the CIO in 1940, but continued as U.M.W. president until 1960.

Rose Schneiderman (1882–1972) was born in Poland and came to this country at the age of eight. She started work at age thirteen in a department store in New York City with a weekly wage of $2.16. Then she worked in a garment factory and embraced socialist ideas during a year in Montreal. She joined the Women's Trade Union League in 1906 and became a full-time organizer. Schneiderman spoke at the funeral for victims of the Triangle Shirtwaist Co. fire, worked for the International Ladies Garment Workers, became president of the New York WTUL, and was appointed to the National Recovery Administration labor advisory board.

Philip Murray (1886–1952) was born in Scotland and came to this country in 1902. He had begun work in the mines at age ten. He was elected president of a U.M.W. local in southwestern Pennsylvania and by 1920 was vice president of the national union under John L. Lewis. He was able to work out a contract with U.S. Steel, but was unable to do the same for what was called the "Little Steel" companies. In addition to the U.M.W. office, he helped to organize the CIO and in 1949 made sure that all Communist-led unions were driven out of the CIO.

Sidney Hillman (1887–1946) was born in Russia, went to England in 1906 and then to this country the following year. He worked in Chicago in clothing manufacture and formed the Amalgamated Clothing Workers of America. In 1914 he moved to New York City and became head of the A.C.W.A. Called a "labor statesman," he supported the "New Deal" and was appointed to a number of positions by President Roosevelt, including the Office of Production Management during the Second World War. Hillman had helped to organize the CIO and became a vice president.

George Meany (1894–1980) grew up in the Bronx, New York City, and became a plumber, soon taking over the management of the union. His business acumen resulted in advancement in the New York building trades, the NY Federation of Labor, and finally the AFL, where he served as secretary-treasurer and then succeeded Green as president. He was a strong anti-Communist and engineered the merger of the AFL and the CIO.

A. Philip Randolph (1898–1979) was born in Crescent City, Florida, but moved to New York City in 1911, when he joined the Socialist Party. He became a sleeping car porter and organized the Black Sleeping Car Porters union in 1925. The union was recognized by the Pullman Co. in 1935, and the porters became an affiliate of the AFL. The National Negro Congress was founded in 1936 with Randolph as president, but he was ousted because of his membership in the Communist Party. Randolph, with the help of Bayard Rustin, planned the 1963 March on Washington for "jobs and freedom," at which Dr. Martin Luther King, Jr. spoke.

Walter Reuther (1907–1970) was born in Wheeling, West Virginia, and became a skilled die and tool maker. He went to work in Detroit for the auto industry and helped to organize the United Auto Workers, which became the largest union in the country. By 1938 he had withdrawn from both the Socialist and Communist Party. Auto executive George Romney called Reuther "the most dangerous man in Detroit." In 1946 he was elected president of the UAW and developed an anti-Communist policy. He became president of the CIO in 1952 and supported the Civil rights movement, participating in the 1963 March on Washington.

Jimmy Hoffa (1913–1975) was born in Indiana and became a leader of the Teamsters in 1932. By 1957 he was the head of one of the most powerful, centralized unions of the time. When a Congressional committee investigated Hoffa, he was convicted of jury tampering, mail and wire fraud, and sentenced to prison. Nixon commuted his sentence, but Hoffa disappeared in 1975.

Cesar Chavez (1927–1993) was born in Arizona and, when his family was evicted from their farm, he joined the host of migrant workers. Because of the influence of a Catholic priest and a community organizer, he began work with the Community Service Organization and developed a policy of non-violence. In 1962 he organized the National Farm Workers Association in California, along with Dolores Huerta and others. The N.F.W.A. became nationally famous through the grape boycott and was chartered by the AFL-CIO.

Selective Bibliography

INTRODUCTION

Bellah, Robert. "Civil Religion in America," *Daedalus*, 96 (1) 1–21

Kathan, Boardman W. "Patriotism, Piety and Pedagogy: Confronting Civil Religion," *Religion Teachers Journal*, 9 (7) 16–19

Lee, Marie Myung-Ok. "Eat Turkey, Become American." *New York Times* (Nov. 26, 2014) A35

Meacham, Jon. *American Gospel: God, the Founding Fathers, and the Making of a Nation.* New York: Random House, 2006

Gorski, Philip. *American Covenant: A History of Civil Religion from the Puritans to the Present.* Princeton, NJ: Princeton University Press, 2017.

Zito, William J. "Thanksgiving Day: Deepening and Strengthening the Secular and the Holy," Unpublished D.Min. diss, Hartford Seminary, 1987

CHAPTER 1—MARTIN LUTHER KING, JR. DAY

Abernathy, Ralph David. *And the Walls Came Tumbling Down.* New York: Harper & Row, 1989

Bontemps, Arna, ed., *Hold Fast to Dreams.* Westchester, IL: Follett, 1969

Branch, Taylor. *At Canaan's Edge: America in the King Years: 1965–1968.* New York: Simon & Schuster, 2006

———. *Parting the Waters: America in the King Years, 1954–1963.* New York: Simon & Schuster, 1988

———. *Pillar of Fire: America in the King Years, 1963–1965.* New York: Simon & Schuster, 1998

Carson, Clayborne. ed., *The Autobiography of Martin Luther King, Jr.,* New York: Warer, 1998

Garrow, David J. *Bearing the Cross: Martin Luther King, Jr. and the Southern Christian Leadership Conference.* New York: William Morrow, 1986

Harding, Vincent. *Martin Luther King: The Inconvenient Hero.* Maryknoll, NY: Orbis 1996

King, Martin Luther, Jr. *The Measure of a Man.* Philadelphia: Christian Education, 1959

———. *Strength to Love.* New York: Harper & Row, 1963

———. *Stride Toward Freedom,* New York: Harper & Row, 1958

———. *Trumpet of Conscience,* New York: Harper & Row, 1968

———. *Where Do We Go From Here: Chaos or Community?* New York: Harper & Row, 1967

———. *Why We Can't Wait.* New York: Harper & Row, 1963

Lewis, John, with Michael D'Orso. *Walking with the Wind: A Memoir of the Movement.* New York: Simon & Schuster, 1998

Oates, Stephen B. *Let the Trumpet Sound.* New York: Harper & Row, 1982

Sitkoff, Harvard. *A Pilgrimage to the Mountaintop.* New York: Hill & Wang, Farrar, Straus & Giroux, 2008

Washington, James M. ed., *A Testament of Hope: The Essential Writings and Speeches of Martin Luther King, Jr.* New York: HarperCollins, 1986

Young, Andrew. *An Easy Burden: The Civil Rights Movement and the Transformation of America.* New York: HarperCollins, 1996

CHAPTER 2—WASHINGTON'S BIRTHDAY, FEBRUARY 22

Abbot, W.W., et.al. *The Papers of George Washington. The Presidential Series, September 1788–March 1797.* Charlottesville, VA: University of Virginia Press, 1989

Boller, John F. Jr. *George Washngton and Religion,* Dallas: Southern Methodist University Press, 1963

Brookhiser, Richard. *Rediscovering George Washington: Founding Father.* New York: Simon & Schuster, 1996

Chernow, Ron. *Washington: A Life.* New York: Penguin, 2010

Connell, Janice. *Faith of Our Founding Father: The Spiritual Journey of George Washington.* New York: Hatherleigh, 2004

Ellis, Joseph J. *His Excellency: George Washington.* New York: Random House, 2004

Ferling, John. *The Ascent of George Washington: The Hidden Political Genious of an American Icon.* New York: Bloomsbury, 2009

Flexner, James Thomas. *George Washington.* Four volumes, Boston, Little, Brown, 1965–1972

———. *Washington, The Indispensable Man.* Boston: Little, Brown, 1974

Freeman, Douglas Southall. *George Washington: A Biography.* Seven volumes, 1948–1957, seventh volume by J.A.Carroll and M.W. Ashworth. New York: Charles Scribner's Sons

Grizzard, Frank E. Jr. *The Ways of Providence: Religion and George Washington.* Charlottesville, VA: Mariner, 2005

Harwell. Richard B. *Washington: An Abridgement in One Volume of the Seven Volumes by Douglas Southall Freeman.* New York: Charles Scribner's Sons, 1968

Lillback, Peter A. *George Washington's Sacred Fire.* Bryn Mawr, PA: Providence Forum, 2006

Novak, Michael and Jana. *Washington's God: Religion, Liberty, and the Father of Our Country.* New York: Perseus, 2006

Roberts, Cokie. *Founding Mothers: The Women Who Raised Our Nation.* New York. NY: HarperCollins, 2004

Ross, Tara and Joseph C. Smith, Jr. *Under God: George Washington and the Question of Church and State.* Dallas: Spence, 2008

Thompson, Mary V. *In The Hands of a Good Providence: Religion in the Life of George Washington.* Charlottesville, VA: University of Virginia Press, 2008

Wiencek, Henry. *An Imperfect God: George Washington, His Slaves, and the Creation of America*. New York Farrar, Straus and Giroux, 2003

CHAPTER 3—MEMORIAL DAY

Catton, Bruce. *The American Heritage New History of the Civil War*. New York: Viking, 1996

———. *The Civil War*. Boston: Houghton & Mifflin, 2004

———. *The Coming Fury,* Garden City, NY: Doubleday, 1961

———. *Never Call Retreat,* Garden City, NY: Doubleday, 1965

———. *Terrible Swift Sword,* Garden City, NY: Doubleday, 1963

Chase, Mary Ellen. "Memorial Day 1900," *Ladies Home Journal.* LXXIV (May 1957) 145

Faust, Drew Gilpin. *This Republic of Suffering: Death and the American Civil War,* New York: Random House, 2008

Foote, Shelby. *The Civil War: A Narrative,* vol. 1, *Fort Sumter to Perryville,* vol. 2, *Fredericksburg to Meridian, Vol. 3, Red River to Appomattox.* New York: Vintage, 1986

Gomez, Joseph L. *Not in Vain: A Story of a Soldier,* Prospect, CT: Biographical, 2007

Lincoln, Abraham. *Speeches and Writings, 1859–1865,* New York: Library of America, 1989

McCrae, John and Andrew MacPhail. *In Flanders Field and Other Poems.* New York: G.P. Putnam, 1919

McPherson, James M. *Battle Cry of Freedom.* New York: Oxford University Press, 1988

Miller, Randall M., Harry S. Stout, and Charles Regan Wilson. eds. *Religion and the American Civil War.* New York: Oxford University Press, 1998

Nevins, Allan. *Ordeal of the Union,* 8 vols. New York: Charles Scribners and Sons, 1947–1965

Noll, Mark A. *The Civil War as a Theological Crisis.* Chapel Hill, NC: University of North Carolina Press, 2006

Ritchey, Russell and Donald Jones. *American Civil Religion.* New York: Harper and Row, 1974

Sandburg, Carl. *Abraham Lincoln: The War Years. Vol II,* New York: Harcourt, Brace, 1926

Stout. Harry S. *Upon the Altar of the Nation: A Moral History of the Civil War.* New York, NY: Viking, 2006

CHAPTER 4—FLAG DAY

Boardman, Henry Decatur. Unpublished letter (Dec. 17, 1862)

D'Otrange Mastai, Boleslaw and Marie-Louise. *The Stars and the Stripes: The American Flag as Art and as History from the Birth of the Republic to the Present.* New York: Alfred A. Knopf, 1973

Furlong, William Rea, Byron McCandless, and Harold D. Langley. *So Proudly We Hail: The History of the United States Flag.* Washington, D.C.: Smithsonian Institution Press, 1981

Guenter, Scot M. *The American Flag, 1777–1924: Cultural Shifts from Creation to Codification.* Rutherford, NJ: Fairleigh Dickinson Press, 1990

Miller, Marla R. *Betsy Ross and the Making of America.* New York: Henry Holt, 2010

Quaife, Milo M., Melvin J. Weig, and Roy E. Appleman. *The History of the United States Flag: From the Revolution To the Present, Including a Guide to its Use and Display.* New York: Harper & Brothers, 1961

Sedeen, Margaret. *Star-Spangled Banner: Our Nation and Its Flag.* Washington, DC: National Geographic Society, 1993

Smith, Whitney. *The Flag Book of the United States.* New York: William Morrow, 1970

Whittier, John Greenleaf. "Barbara Frietchie." *A Library of Poetry and Song.* New York, NY: J.B. Ford, 1872, 448

CHAPTER 5—INDEPENDENCE DAY—FOURTH OF JULY

Beeman, Richard R. *Our Lives, Our Fortunes, and Our Sacred Honor: The Forging of American Independence. 1774-1776.* New York: Basic, 2013

Becker, Carl L. *The Declaration of Independence: A Study in the History of Political Ideas.* New York: Alfred A. Knopf, Inc. 1942

Douglass, Frederick. *Oration, Delivered in Corinthian Hall, Rochester.* Rochester: Lee, Mann, 1852

Maier, Pauline. *American Scripture: Making the Declaration of Independence,* New York: Alfred A. Knopf, 1997

———. Editor and Introduction, *The Declaration of Independence and the Constitution of the United States,* New York: Bantam Classic, Random House, 1998

Redding, Rev. David. "The Faith of Our Fathers," *Life* (June 30, 1961) 52

Shuffelton, Frank. *Letters of John and Abigail Adams.* New York: Penquin, 2003

CHAPTER 6—LABOR DAY

Debs, Eugene. *DEBS: His Life, Writings and Speeches.* Gerard, KS: Appeal to Reason, 1908

Dray, Philip. *There is Power in a Union: The Epic Story of Labor in America.* New York: Doubleday, Random House, 2010

Dubofsky, Melvin and Warren Van Tine. *Labor Leaders in America.* Urbana and Chicago: University of Illinois Press, 1987

Dubofsky, Melvin and Foster R. Dulles. *Labor in America: A History,* 6th Edition. Wheeling, IL: Harlan Davidson, 1999

Gorn, Elliott J. *Mother Jones: The Most Dangerous Woman in America.* New York: Hill and Wang, 2001

Green, James. *Death in the Haymarket: A Story of Chicago, the First Labor Movement and the Bombing That Divided Gilded Age America.* New York: Pantheon, Random House, 2006

Honey, Michael K, ed. *All Labor Has Dignity.* Boston: Beacon, 2011

LeBlanc, Paul. *A Short History of the United States Working Class: From Colonial Times to the 21st Century.* Amherst, NY: Humanity, 1999

Lichtenstein, Nelson. *State of the Union: A Century of American Labor.* Princeton, NJ: Princeton University Press, 2002

The Little Red Song Book. 36th edition. Ypsilanti, MI: Industrial Workers of the World, 1995

Meltzer, Milton. *Bread and Roses: The Struggle of American Labor, 1865–1915.* New York: Alfred A. Knopf, 1967

Murolo, Priscilla and A.B.Chitty. *From the Folks Who Brought You the Weekend: A Short, Illustrated History of Labor in the United States.* New York: The New Press, 2001

Terkel, Studs. *Working: People Talk About What They Do all Day and How They Feel About What They Do.* New York: Ballantine, 1985

Wertheimer, Barbara Mayer. *We Were There: The Story of Working Women in America.* New York: Pantheon, 1977

Zinn, Howard. *A People's History of the United States.* New York: HarperCollins, 1980

CHAPTER 7—CONSTITUTION DAY AND CITIZENSHIP DAY, SEPTEMBER 17

Beeman, Richard. *Plain, Honest Men: The Making of the American Constitution.* New York: Random House, 2009

Berkin, Carol. *A Brilliant Solution: Inventing the American Constitution.* New York: Crown, 1987

Bowen, Catherine Drinker. *Miracle at Philadelphia: The Story of the Constitutional Convention, May to September 1787.* Boston: Little, Brown and Company, 1966

Breyer, Stephen. *Making Our Democracy Work: A Judge's View.* New York: Alfred A. Knopf, 2010

Chidsey, Donald Barr. *The Birth of the Constitution: An Informal History.* New York: Crown, 1964

Collier, Christopher and James Lincoln. *Decision at Philadelphia: The Constitutional Convention of 1787.* New York: Random House, 1986

Farrand, Max, ed. *The Records of the Federal Convention of 1787.* New Haven, CT: Yale University Press, 1966

Ketcham, Ralph. ed. *The Anti-Federalist Papers and the Constitutional Convention Debates.* New York: Penguin Putnam, 1986

Maier, Pauline. *Ratification: The People Debate the Constitution, 1787–1788.* New York: Simon & Schuster, 2010

Marshall, Thurgood. "Reflections on the Bicentennial of the United States Constitution," *Harvard Law Review* 101 (1) 1–5

Morris, Richard B. *Witnesses at the Creation: Hamilton, Madison, Jay and the Constitution.* New York: Holt, Rinehart & Winston, 1985

Peters, William. *A More Perfect Union: The Making of the United States Constitution of 1787.* New York: Crown, 1987

Rossiter, Clinton. *The Federalist Papers.* New York: Penquin, 1961

———. *The Grand Convention.* New York: Macmillan, 1966

Stewart, David O. *The Summer of 1787: The Men Who Invented the Constitution.* New York: Simon & Schuster, 2007

Wood, Gordon S. *The Making of the Constitution.* Waco, TX: Baylor University Press, 1987

Wood, James E. "No Religious Test Shall Ever Be Required: Reflections on the Bicentennial of the U.S. Constitution," *Journal of Church and State.* 29 (2) 199–208

CHAPTER 8—COLUMBUS DAY

Bergreen, Laurence. *Columbus: The Four Voyages.* New York: Viking/Penguin, 2011
Deagan, Kathleen A. "La Isabela, Europe's First Foothold in the New World," *National Geographic,* 181 (1) 40–53
Dor-Ner, Zvi. *Columbus and the Age of Discovery.* New York: William Morrow, 1991
Fuson, Robert H. *The Log of Christopher Columbus.* Camden, Maine: International Marine, 1987
Judge, Joseph. "Our Search for the True Columbus Landfall," *National Geographic,* 170 (5) 566–599
Lyon, Eugene. "Search for Columbus," *National Geographic,* 181 (1) 2–39
Morison, Samuel Eliot. *Admiral of the Ocean Sea: A Life of Christopher Columbus.* Boston: Little, Brown, 1942
Wilford, John Noble. *The Mysterious History of Columbus: An Exploration of the Man, the Myth, the Legacy.* New York: Alfred A. Knopf, 1991

CHAPTER 9—VETERANS DAY

Brokaw, Tom. *An Album of Memories: Personal Histories from the Greatest Generation.* New York: Random House, 2001
———. *The Greatest Generation.* New York: Random House, 1998
———. *The Greatest Generation Speaks: Letters and Reflections.* New York: Random House, 1999
Childers, Thomas. *Soldier From the War Returning: The Greatest Generation's Troubled Homecoming from World War II.* Boston: Houghton Mifflin, 2009
Collins, Julia. *My Father's War: A Memoir.* New York: Four Walls Eight Windows, 2002
Coyne, Kevin. *Marching Home: To War and Back with the Men of One American Town.* New York: Penguin Putnam, 2003
Mathews, Tom. *Our Fathers' War: Growing Up in the Shadow of the Greatest Generation.* New York: Broadway, 2005
Pyle, Ernie. *Brave Men.* New York: Henry Holt, 1944
Rose, Kenneth D. *Myth and the Greatest Generation: A Social History of Americans in World War II.* New York: Routledge, Taylor & Francis, 2008
Rubin, Richard. *The Last of the Doughboys: The Forgotten Generation and Their Forgotten World War.* Boston: Houghton Mifflin Harcourt, 2013
———. "Over There and Gone Forever." *New York Times* (Nov. 12, 2007) A21
Van Ells, Mark D. *To Hear Only Thunder Again: America's World War II Veterans Come Home.* Lanham, MD: Lexington, 2001

CHAPTER 10—THANKSGIVING DAY

Appelbaum, Diana Karter. *Thanksgiving: An American Holiday, An American History.* New York: Facts on File, 1984

Baker, James W. *Thanksgiving: The Biography of a American Holiday.* Durham, NH: University of New Hampshire Press, 2009

Bradford, William. *Of Plymouth Plantation,* 1620–1647. New York: Alfred A. Knopf, 1952

Colman, Penny. *Thanksgiving: The True Story.* New York: Henry Holt, 2008

Grace, Catherine O'Neill and Margaret M. Bruchac. *1621: A New Look at Thanksgiving.* Washington, DC: National Geographic Society, 2004

Hale, Sarah Josepha. *Northwood, or, Life North and South,* New York: H. Long & Brother, 1852

Heath, Dwight B. ed., *A Journal of the Pilgrims at Plymouth (Mourt's Relation),* New York: Corinth, 1963

Hodgson, Godfrey. *A Great and Godly Adventure: The Pilgrims and the Myth of the First Thanksgiving.* New York: Public Affairs, 2006

Kirkpatrick, Melanie. *Thanksgiving: The Holiday at the Heart of the American Experience.* New York: Encounter, 2016

Linton, Ralph and Adelin. *We Gather Together: The Story of Thanksgiving.* New York: Henry Schuman, 1949

Love, William DeLoss. *Fast and Thanksgiving Days of New England.* Boston: Houghton Mifflin, 1895

Philbrick, Nathaniel. *Mayflower: A Story of Courage, Community, and War.* New York: Viking Penguin, 2006

Shapiro, Walter. "Why We've Failed to Ruin Thanksgiving." *Time* (Nov. 27, 1989) 94

Travers, Carolyn Freeman. ed. *The Thanksgiving Primer.* Plymouth, MA: Plimouth Plantation, 1987, 1991

Willison, George F. *Saints and Strangers.* New York: Reynal and Hitchcock, 1945. (Reprinted 1964 by *Time*)

Zito, William J. "Thanksgiving Day: Deepening and Strengthening the Secular and the Holy," Unpublished D.Min. diss. Hartford Seminary, 1987

APPENDIX A—ABRAHAM LINCOLN'S BIRTHDAY

Kathan, Boardman W. "Lincoln's Birthday Should Be a Federal Holiday," *For The People,* 17 (4) 1–2

Lincoln, Abraham, *Speeches and Writings,* 1859–1865. New York: Library of America, 1989 106–108, 160–167

Index

A

B

C

F

I

M

N

O

P

S

T

U

V

W

Y

Z

About the Author

BOARDMAN W. KATHAN, a native of New Haven, Connecticut, received the B.A. degree from Wesleyan University and the M.Div. from Yale University Divinity School. He was ordained by the Chicago Association of the Congregational Christian Churches and served churches in Connecticut, Illinois, and Minnesota. He worked on the staff of a state conference in Boston, a national board in New York City, and for many years was the executive of an inter-faith, international organization, the Religious Education Association (R.E.A.). For twenty-five years he was the archivist of the R.E.A., and the resulting archive collections are located at Yale. He taught in the Sociology Department of Emerson College, Boston, for a semester, and for two years in a field-based course at Yale Divinity School.

The author has done graduate study at the University of Connecticut, New York University, and Hartford Seminary. He was awarded a Fulbright Scholarship in 1952-1953 and studied at the University of Leiden, the Netherlands, where he continued his interest in the Dutch theologian, Jacobus Arminius, who modified the strict theology of John Calvin. The movement, Arminianism, influenced John Milton, John Locke, the Methodists, and the Latitudinarian or moderate wing of the Anglican church.

Among his many writings are curriculum books, a special issue of the journal, *Religious Education*, a memoir titled *My Prospects*, and the history of a local church, which won the Fagley Award from the Congregational Christian Historical Society as the best resource in the country for churches of a particular size. His essay on the religion of John Quincy Adams won first prize from the Historical Council of the United Church of Christ and was published in the denomination's journal *Prism*. He has written many articles, chapters in books, and online entries, has edited monographs, and has been recorded in a cassette tape series.

He married Joyce M. Clark of Middletown, Connecticut, and the couple had three children (one deceased) and four grandchildren. His home is in Prospect, Connecticut, where he is active as a member and past treasurer of the local Land Trust and as the past historian of the Prospect Congregational Church. He had previously served as a member and chairman of the Region 16 Board of Education and the secretary of the local Bicentennial Commission.